"As the CEO of a billion-dollar IT services company, I am on a journey to be in the path of relevance to our customers in their digital transformation. The idea of weaving our connections for network orchestration is very appealing. I couldn't put this book down. Very structured, practical, and thought provoking. Now I'm ready to PIVOT. A must-read for all CXOs with inquisitive minds."

—**GANESH AYYAR**, CEO, Mphasis

"As the world becomes increasingly digital, organizations need not just digitize, or even transform, but rather digitally reinvent themselves. Values are shifting increasingly to the network. The orchestrators of such networks increasingly get more of the value from the ecosystem and businesses they support. Assets, services, or technology cannot compete with the benefits of the network provider.

The authors of *The Network Imperative* do a great job of laying out the competitive advantages of network-based organizations operating in the open-platform digital world and how they will impact every industry. The authors explain the rationale behind the network business model—its value creation as well as its tendency toward exponential growth.

The book provides the promise of value enhancement and wealth, as well the principles of success, the PIVOT process to get you there, and the practices and mental models required. If you are part of the *Fortune* 1000 and want to be there ten years from now, you need to listen to what these authors have to say in this important book."

—**SAUL BERMAN**, Vice President and Chief Strategist, IBM Global Business Services

"Interdependencies and how to recognize them, allocate resources between them, and optimize them will define success in our new networked economy and operational models. We all need guidance and access to wisdom on how to win in a networked, interdependent system. *The Network Imperative* will help us to be more effective system thinkers, with Barry, Megan, and Jerry guiding the way."

—**PHIL COWDELL**, CEO, MediaCom North America

"Get ready for a future in which everyone and everything are digitally connected, marginal costs approach zero, and openness to the ideas and assets that exist around the organization matter more than sheer scale. The successful firms of the future will embrace the principles for creating network value found in this prescient book."

—**GEORGE DAY**, Geoffrey T. Boisi Professor, Emeritus, the Wharton School

"In the new world of crowd sourcing, the sharing economy, and the internet of everything, there is no question that every business is being transformed by a networked world. In *The Network Imperative*, Libert, Beck, and Wind break down this twenty-first century phenomenon and offer an actionable and effective approach for any business to not only ward off disintermediation, but also to set a path for long-term success."

—**MICHAEL DISTEFANO**, Senior Vice President and CMO, Korn Ferry; President, Korn Ferry Institute

"Networks really are at the heart of our modern economic system. A model spurred by the eponymic GAFA (Google, Amazon, Facebook, Apple) but also encompassing billion-dollar unicorns and all other companies changing our lives through computer technology, *The Network Imperative* not only reveals the strategic value of networks but also delivers an actionable framework to help industry leaders transform asset-based companies into graph-powered organizations."

—**STÉPHANE DISTINGUIN**, founder and CEO, FABERNOVEL

"Digital innovations are coming on fast and furious. But to flourish they need a much sounder business model. Read all about it in this very well researched and insightful book."

—**AMITAI ETZIONI**, author, *Privacy in a Cyber Age*

"As a pioneer of the Network Age, I found this book to be an understandable and valuable help in the integration of digital technology into the business world. All too often technologists do not have a clear understanding of how our systems impact and affect the organization. The book provides a complete and structured guide to the impact of new technology on organizations. As a longtime consultant to businesses, established and start-up, I strongly recommend this book to all participants in this evolving restructuring of the world."

—**DAVE FARBER**, Alfred Fitler Moore Professor of Telecommunication Systems, Emeritus, University of Pennsylvania

"When the internet burst onto the scene, many business leaders were in denial about its ultimate impact. Denial then gave way to a sense of uncertainty—the risk (fear) of disruption. Disruption has now clearly yielded to opportunity—opportunity that inspires creativity, demands reinvention, and offers the prospect of major new business success. *The Network Imperative* will disturb the complacent but energize those who are capable of inventing the future, and they will be the winners."

—**GREG FARRINGTON**, former Dean, School of Engineering and Applied Science, University of Pennsylvania

"*The Network Imperative* offers very practical advice for companies struggling to find their way in the digital revolution. The 'Ten Strategies for Creating Network Value' are relevant to both long-established brands and those still establishing their identity. A valuable tool kit!"

—**DON GAGNON**, CEO, AAA Club Partners

"How to value an organization or an individual? What candidate to hire for a position, whom to select as a mentor in a corporation or as a thesis adviser in college? It's the strength of their network, stupid! This truth should inform all aspects of decision making, from long-range corporate strategy to everyday judgment calls. I enjoyed reading this insightful and timely book, aware that it addresses one of the most fundamental facts of today's life."

—**EDUARDO D. GLANDT**, former Dean, School of Engineering and Applied Science, University of Pennsylvania

"Every manager and consumer knows they live through fast-changing business paradigms but are often at a loss when trying to make sense of the digital and network revolutions taking place around them. We need a framework to understand what's going on and predict how things can develop. We also need to separate the facts from the hype. This is what *The Network Imperative* delivers to its readers in a clear and compelling manner."

—**GABRIEL HAWAWINI**, Henry Grunfeld Chaired Professor of Investment Banking, Professor of Finance, and former Dean, INSEAD

"Business models based on digital networks will be generating vast value in the years ahead, but only to those who comprehend the challenges and activate the opportunities. To do so will require new styles of leadership—from the boardroom on down through the entire organization. All this is compellingly analyzed in *The Network Imperative.* This indeed is your playbook for being a winner in the digital revolution."

—**JIM KRISTIE**, Editor, *Directors & Boards*

"Ninety-eight percent of the businesses in the world are non-digital. By the year 2020, most of these enterprises risk becoming prey for digital business network predators, with severe social and economic consequences.

This fascinating book provides an important wake-up call for the leaders of these non-digital, non-networked enterprises, large or small. The book provides a comprehensive analysis of the new digital, networked world and describes it as one with unlimited growth potential, subject to the law of increasing returns. In this networked ecosystem, every human being is a potential source of creativity and innovation,

an important node in the network, and capable of contributing both tangible and non-tangible assets. These assets can have significant economic value if provided with the proper platforms, some of which are already available and are integrating cloud data with big data analytics and abundant access.

The authors provide a blueprint for business leaders as to how to transform their enterprises to operate successfully in the digital, networked world. They outline concrete steps leaders must take to gain a renewed understanding of their organizations, as all aspects of business structure and management must be transformed in a networked organization. The authors base their analysis on comprehensive academic research and many real-world examples.

This fascinating book is a must-read for all those responsible for the well-being of their organizations and, ultimately, for the well-being of their employees and customers. I read it in one go!"

—**NOAM LEMELSHTRICH LATAR**, founding Dean, Sammy Ofer School of Communications, Interdisciplinary Center, Herzliya, Israel

"For organizations serving those most in need, I believe that digital networks—which are tearing down the traditional confines of geographic barriers—have the potential to increase our impact by ten or even a hundred times. There is no limit, which this book brilliantly demonstrates."

—**TERRI LUDWIG**, President and CEO, Enterprise Community Partners

"Very well-researched book with a strong message. A must-read."

—**VIJAY MAHAJAN**, John P. Harbin Centennial Chair in Business, McCombs School of Business, University of Texas at Austin

"Many organizations are struggling with digitalizing their businesses for fear of being disrupted by insurgents with new business models and technologies from the network economy. This book lays out ten principles and five practical steps to help businesses reap full benefit from the convergence of technologies in the digital age. A must-read for leaders who want to stay relevant."

—**TAN CHIN NAM**, senior corporate adviser; retired Permanent Secretary, Singapore Public Service

"The authors identify what people feel is true but can't describe: that the world around them is changing as we become more connected and aware. Companies with connectedness in their DNA have captured enormous value as they have disrupted

incumbents. They have collaborated to create products and services that are far superior to what their own smartest people thought were best for their customers. Companies that maintain their arrogance in the face of revolution are up against a persistent and formidable force that is unlikely to be reversed. What we are seeing is just the beginning."

—**BRUCE NEWMAN**, Partner, Entrepreneur Partners, L.P.

"No doubt the digital impact will change many business models. The study of this impact is a requirement for everybody involved in business, from the operations level through the governance level. The work of Barry Libert, Megan Beck, and Jerry Wind is excellent and easy to read while rigorous and based on well-structured research. I have known Jerry for many years, and he has been the leading pioneer of network-centered organizations."

—**PEDRO NUENO**, Professor of Entrepreneurship, Emeritus, IESE Business School, University of Navarra

"I have been on a number of major corporate boards, and I am now in the private equity business. I believe that *The Network Imperative* is a must-read for board members and investors."

—**RUSSELL E. PALMER**, former Dean, the Wharton School; former CEO, Touche Ross (now Deloitte Touche Tohmatsu Limited)

"*The Network Imperative* is a must-read because professional relationships, business models, and the way we position value in only three to five years will be changed to a point that is difficult to grasp. Lead the change in your company, or be prepared to eat dust."

—**JEROME PERIBERE**, President and CEO, Sealed Air

"Today's management education is focused on the firm. It is clear that networks like Uber, Airbnb, and Amazon require us to rethink management education if our future leaders are to have any chance of survival and growth. *The Network Imperative* is a must-read for all business, public policy, and academic leaders—today's and tomorrow's."

—**DAVID C. SCHMITTLEIN**, John C. Head III Dean, MIT Sloan School of Management

"One of the most insightful and practical books on how networks are creating future competitive advantage. Among the ten tenets of the network advantage (for example, from physical to digital and from tangible to intangible), I really liked what a company can do to treat its customers as contributors, employees as partners, and board members as stakeholder representatives."

—**JAGDISH SHETH**, Charles H. Kellstadt Professor of Marketing, Goizueta Business School, Emory University

"Understanding digital networks and driving your organization toward the network orchestrator business model is simply a matter of survival in today's environment of hyper change. No business, large or small, is immune. *The Network Imperative* does an excellent job of explaining these concepts and, more importantly, providing the process to guide implementation in your organization. Do not wait until it is too late for your business. Get started today!"

—**DOUG SMITH**, former Division Controller, Hardware Engineering, Apple

"The next wave of innovation is upon us. It's networks. Networks that need orchestration to extract the promised value. *The Network Imperative* spells it out with crystal clarity. Here's how the world is changing because of networks; here's how to create a network business model; and here's how to lead one. Take the plunge to reinvent your business or risk withering away in irrelevance. A must-read."

—**ALFRED P. WEST JR.**, Chairman and CEO, SEI

THE NETWORK IMPERATIVE

THE NETWORK IMPERATIVE

HOW TO SURVIVE *and* GROW *in the* AGE *of* DIGITAL BUSINESS MODELS

BARRY LIBERT
MEGAN BECK
JERRY WIND

Harvard Business Review Press
Boston, Massachusetts

Printed in the United States of America

10 9 8 7 6 5 4 3 2 1

Library of Congress Cataloging-in-Publication Data

Names: Libert, Barry, author. | Beck, Megan, author. | Wind, Yoram, author.
Title: The network imperative : how to survive and grow in the age of digital business models / Barry D. Libert with Megan Beck and Yoram (Jerry) Wind.
Description: Boston, Massachusetts : Harvard Business Review Press, [2016]
Identifiers: LCCN 2016014992 | ISBN 9781633692053 (alk. paper)
Subjects: LCSH: Electronic commerce. | Business enterprises—Computer networks. | Industrial management—Computer networks.
Classification: LCC HF5548.32 .L5227 2016 | DDC 658.8/72—dc23 LC record available at https://lccn.loc.gov/2016014992

ISBN: 978-1-63369-205-3
eISBN: 978-1-63369-206-0

The paper used in this publication meets the requirements of the American National Standard for Permanence of Paper for Publications and Documents in Libraries and Archives Z39.48-1992.

Dedications

To my wife, who taught me the power of love
To my two sons, who taught me the value of life
To my friends, who taught me the importance of kindness

—Barry Libert

To my mother, my lifelong reference point for
both greatness and practicality

—Megan Beck

To my invaluable networks:
To my reverse mentors—children, granddaughter, students, and staff
To my friends, colleagues, clients, and research collaborators
To my beloved late wife, Dina, whose love and inspiration
have accompanied me throughout my life

—Jerry Wind

Special Thanks

Susan Corso
for her insight and editing

George Calapai
for his inspired digital platform

CONTENTS

A CALL TO ACTION

The Digital Revolution gets all the headlines these days. But turning slowly beneath the fast-forward turbulence . . . is a much more profound revolution—the Network Economy.

—Kevin Kelly, founder, *Wired* magazine

HISTORY HAS CROSSED A CRITICAL INFLECTION POINT. THE formal frameworks used to design and structure firms, lead, govern, and value them are becoming obsolete.

The driving force behind this accelerating change is a shift from *tangible to intangible, physical to digital, and firm-based to network-based business models.* A network is a set of connections that enables people or things to connect, share information, and exchange products, services, or insights. The primary law of networks is that value expands exponentially with the number of connections within the network. With the growth of digital platforms, organizations can now expand their network connections rapidly and at very low cost.

Today's leading organizations are network-centric and are creating remarkable economic returns by capitalizing on network advantages, such as co-creation with their customers (Facebook); digital platforms (Amazon); shared assets (Uber and Airbnb); and big data insights (Netflix and Google). Leaders and investors who want to participate in the network revolution need to envision their future, and the future of their industry, based on intangibles and networks or risk falling behind.

The Network Imperative provides the why and how to survive and thrive in the age of hyperscale digital networks. It defines the *ten principles for network organizations and a five-step process for pivoting* your organization toward today's most valuable and profitable business models. Join the network movement online at openmatters.com.

THE PROMISE

PART ONE

The Value Is in the Network

DIGITAL NETWORKS ARE EATING THE WORLD

Why is it so difficult for established companies to pull off the new growth that business model innovation can bring? Here's why: they don't understand their current business model well enough to know if it would suit a new opportunity or hinder it, and they don't know how to build a new model when they need it.

—Clayton M. Christensen, author, *The Innovator's Dilemma*

DIGITAL NETWORKS ARE CHANGING ALL THE RULES OF BUSINESS. It is clear that new, scalable, digital, and industry-hopping business models, like those of Amazon, Google, Uber, and Airbnb, are affecting growth, scale, and profit potential for companies across the board. Investors are already shifting capital toward the latest business models. The question isn't whether your organization needs to change, but when and how much.

Established non-digital, non-network business models make up more than 98 percent of the market and have a lot of work to do. Most of these companies are racing to update their strategy, leadership, technology, and organizational design, but the performance gap is widening. This book is intended to help those firms that are not digital start-ups or technology superstars bridge the gap and create unprecedented growth and value in the age of hyperscale digital networks.

You may feel that network disruption is a distant concern for your business or irrelevant for your industry, and that you have more-pressing concerns, but be aware: investor capital, customer revenue and affinity, top talent, and market buzz are shifting away from established firms toward network organizations. Further, our research indicates that digital networks are entering almost every industry, even some of the most mundane. Consider a few striking examples of industries that have been turned upside down by digital networks—where young upstarts, many of which are still private, are rapidly outperforming established firms.

These companies, with digital network business models, have sent shockwaves through their respective industries, and, remarkably,

Network firms versus traditional firms

Network firms	Market value	Traditional firms	Market value
Uber	• $60–70B valuation • No cars, more than 1M drivers	Hertz	• $7B market cap • Estimated 350K cars
Airbnb	• $24B valuation • 1.5M+ homes for rent, none owned	Starwood	• $12.2B purchase price in Nov. 2015 • 1,270+ hotel properties
WeChat	• $84B estimated value • 650M users • 0 miles network fiber	AT&T	• $207B market cap • 122M phone subscribers • 1M miles of network fiber
Alibaba	• $200B market cap • 0 retail locations	Walmart	• $190B market cap • 11,000 retail locations

they did it without the traditional assets considered requirements for success. Our work with boards and leaders, as well as our angel investing in start-ups, has shown us that a key differentiator between network firms and traditional firms is the thinking of the leadership team. Network leaders think differently about value and value creation. In fact, their thinking is the opposite of many traditional business beliefs.

What does the opposite thinking of these network leaders look like? Here are a few examples.

- Traditional leaders ask what value their firm can provide. *Network leaders ask what value their customers and other networks have to offer.*
- Traditional leaders think the goal is to sell more products to customers. *Network leaders see the value in customer co-creation, advocacy, and sharing.*
- Traditional leaders think they're operating at full capacity. *Network leaders see the world differently and full of additional potential.*

This different thinking helps digital network leaders see and invest in a world of abundance, where there are excess assets everywhere, both tangible and intangible. Whether these assets are houses, cars, photos, knowledge, skills, or networks, there are people in the world willing to share them in order to earn money, garner recognition for their expertise, or connect their stories and experiences to the world around them.

In contrast, most organizations believe they're working at or near full capacity. Most business leaders believe that the only way to generate more value is to make, market, and sell more of what they have or do. But that old thinking limits their profitability and growth. Many of our most admired companies won't stand a chance when the most valuable digital networks take on their markets. Nigel Fenwick of Forrester

Research said that by 2020, every organization will be either digital predator or digital prey.[1]

Your Strategy Needs a Business Model Face-Lift

To return to the quote by Clayton Christensen at the start of this chapter, the problem is that most organizations don't know where they are starting, much less where they are headed and how to get there. We wrote this book to help the leaders of traditional firms—those focused internally on using *their own* assets and employees to make, market, and sell—enter the world of digital network business models and leverage an external network to contribute its assets, ideas, skills, and relationships and share in the value created. Savvy investors and employees will also find that business model perspective is useful in allocating their capital and energy.

This book began twenty years ago, when Barry Libert, a strategist by background, was researching the sources of value and their migration from tangible to intangible. His first book on value was called *Cracking the Value Code*, and his research resulted in a simple finding: that traditional beliefs about value were wrong. One such belief was that physical things, such as real estate and equipment, should be accounted as secure and enduring assets, whereas the people who built, managed, and used those assets should be accounted as expenses. Now we realize that whereas physical assets often depreciate, people assets often appreciate—increasing in skills, knowledge, and value over time. This is just as true for customers, properly cared for, as it is for employees. Consider the value of Facebook, whose 1.6 billion customers create all the content for the platform, acting as both contributors and subscribers.

At around the same time that Libert was researching value at a large consulting firm, Jerry Wind, a senior faculty member at University of Pennsylvania's Wharton School, was researching how firms were organized. Wind's work on network organizations versus traditional firms resulted in the formation of the SEI Research Center at Wharton.

The two men met in 2001 and together started examining how the beliefs of leaders and boards shaped the actions and outcomes of firms, including their organizational design and financial performance. Libert's book on networks was called *We Are Smarter Than Me*, and Wind's, *The Network Challenge*.

In 2013, Libert partnered with Megan Beck, who applied her experience analyzing complex problems and managing organizations through change to explore this dramatic shift, document what it means for legacy organizations, and create a practical guidebook for change. Over the past several years these authors, along with a team of researchers, writers, and technologists, have worked to create this thinking, this book, and the accompanying digital platform.

The team examined the S&P 1500 index, which includes large-cap, mid-cap, and small-cap companies, over a forty-year time horizon, seeking to understand how capital allocation, business models, and economic outcomes were changing with the digital and network revolutions. Their findings are included here. But this book is much more than just research about business models. It also shows you what to do, and how to do it, in order to achieve growth and value in a world dominated by digital networks. In short, your existing strategy and organizational design need a business model face-lift.

Adopt New Thinking

The way most of the world thinks about assets is wrong. Physical assets, the darlings of the Industrial Revolution and the basis of today's largest firms, depreciate, become obsolete, can be destroyed by flood and fire, are expensive to move, and aren't capable of innovation (because, after all, they don't think). People, on the other hand, have a lot of potential. Whether employees, customers, or partners, people can generate new ideas, solve problems on their own, promote and share brands, and serve various other functions. With proper training or cultivation, people appreciate, rather than depreciate, in value to your organization.

Sometimes leaders make a mistake by thinking they've captured the value of people by hiring them as employees or gaining them as customers. This view is simply too narrow. Our consumer spending and our efforts at work represent only slivers of our overall capabilities and assets. Most employees are hired to do a specific job in a specific way; ask yourself how many of your own jobs have accessed your full potential for innovation and productivity. Consider how Airbnb has gained far more than the revenue from lodging rentals. It has accessed the underutilized resources of entire populations—resources that simply were wasted before.

The internet spelled the demise of closed-source business models based on physical assets. For example, Wikipedia and its network of unpaid contributors disrupted a 250-year-old company called Encyclopedia Britannica. Since then, millennials are turning to Yelp instead of Zagat for a restaurant recommendation, to Angie's List instead of Yellow Pages for service providers, and to LinkedIn rather than a headhunter when they need a job. These digital, open-source, open-platform business models are creating new, exponential insights and connections that yield extraordinary value. Consequently, the emerging power of networks presents new risks for established firms in all industries.

We are at the beginning of a rapid upending of traditional ways of creating value, and it is occurring in every industry. Firm-centric organizations that use their own resources to create and keep all the value for themselves are slowly being replaced by those that share value creation with networks of individuals connected by digital technologies. And these new network-centric businesses offer many economic advantages.

Make It Valuable and Practical

In preparing to write this book and document our research, we regularly heard the same refrain: whatever you do, make it practical and actionable, with the emphasis on actionable. As long-standing authors, advis-

ers, and investors, we have heard the refrain from those we work with: "We get the message. There is work to do—but *how* do we actually do it? Most of the companies you and others write about (such as Uber, Airbnb, Alibaba, and Etsy) were born as digital networks. They never had to upend their existing business model and become something other than what they are. The rest of us need practical advice and tools so that we can compete, grow, and prosper."

So we bring this book down quickly from the high-level research to the practical how-tos. Whether you make widgets, provide services, or offer technologies, whether you lead a billion-dollar corporation or a family business, we will help you join the digitally networked world. We have worked hard to make this a *how-to* book, not a *why-to* book.

In part I, "The Promise," we share our research on business models (from firm-centric to network-centric models) and discuss how investing capital in network business models has a dramatic impact on economic value creation.

In part II, "The Principles," we examine how network organizations operate differently from traditional organizations. Each principle represents a significant shift from the legacy firm to the network organization. You can use these ten principles as levers to accelerate your transition to augmenting your business with the networks that exist around it.

In part III, "The PIVOT," we share our PIVOT process—five specific steps that you can take, beginning Monday morning, to plant the seeds of digital networks within your own organization and set the path for greater co-creation and shared rewards. Adopting a new business model is not easy, and it is not simple, but these steps will help you define what you need and identify how to implement it in a practical sequence.

In part IV, "The Practice," we examine what it takes to lead a digital network organization and help you examine the unstated and unrealized mental models that guide your thoughts, actions, investments, and ultimately your organization's future. We will also discuss what it means to you to be the leader in your own network.

Anticipate a Great Future Ahead

No transition is easy. But our playbook is intended to help leaders create fertile ground for previously unachievable growth, profit, and value. Remember that your organization and your network participants will share this value. In the network age, you cannot do this on your own. Partnering with a network requires actual partnership—a mutual arrangement from which both parties benefit.

Although you could take a mercenary approach, trying to extract as much value as you can from your network, be aware that network members are beginning to see what they bring to the table. The articles they write for LinkedIn, the art they sell on Etsy, and the content they generate for TripAdvisor have value. They want to share in the value, and they will find partners who will let them. In return, they will reward their partners with loyalty, advocacy, information, and assets.

In short, digital networks are changing *what* we do, *how* we do it, and *who* gets rewarded. There is great untapped value in networks, and this book will help you on your journey to becoming a network leader and firm. It gives you the research to motivate you, the principles to guide you, and the practices that will ensure your success.

Doing the hard work and realizing the value of digital networks in your organization—well, that's your job.

Join the network movement to access our digital tools, audit your business model, and create a plan for growth at openmatters.com.

NETWORKS HAVE BIG ADVANTAGES

In the network economy, success is self-reinforcing: it obeys the law of increasing returns.

—Kevin Kelly, founder, *Wired* magazine

CONNECTING THINGS CREATES GREAT POWER. A LINK, A CHANnel, a highway—all act as permanent conduits over which many things can flow. Networks, pathways between many nodes, have always been important to the economy. Consider the US interstate highway system, which was authorized by President Eisenhower in 1956. As the system spread across the country, connecting cities and towns, workers and farmers, it facilitated a great flow of things—physical things like oil, machinery, and goods, and also people, with their services and ideas. Once the backbone was built, a steady stream of new things, people, and ideas percolated around the United States. The course of this stream was determined by the users, reacting to cultural shifts and market forces. What a marvel!

Building the highway system, however, was a vast, expensive, and difficult undertaking. As a big, heavy, physical *thing*, it did not scale quickly or easily. The construction took thirty-five years and an estimated $425 billion (in 2006 dollars). In contrast, Facebook grew to 500 million users in just over six years. Digital technology makes all the difference. Not only are many of the most valuable goods in our market—such as ideas, intellectual capital, and communication—digitizable, but also our digital networks allow them to proliferate with great ease. The scaling cost is nearly zero.

And remember the other powerful characteristic of networks that has driven their phenomenal growth: networks are subject to the law of increasing returns. The value in networks is found in the connectivity between nodes, and every additional node increases the value of the network exponentially. Telephones are the classic example. The more people who have them, the more people you can reach with convenience. In terms of digital assets, each new member on Facebook is a potential new friend for every member in the network. Each new seller on eBay creates a new pool of goods for every eBay shopper. Each new freelancer on Upwork is a potential worker for every hiring client on the site.

Because of the law of increasing returns, networks are designed for growth—and by this we mean that the human beings who make up any network are, by their nature and the nature of the network, incentivized to grow it. As a network expands, whether a network of people, sensors, or information, the benefit provided to each node accelerates radically upward, and that fuels additional growth. And when this growth comes at nearly zero marginal cost . . . well, that's why digital networks are expanding at an industry-gobbling pace.

The Numbers Tell the Story

We clearly identified the advantages of digital network business models from our observations in working with clients and investing in startups, but we needed proof beyond empirical evidence to bring these ideas

to the market. For that reason, we began a multiyear, in-depth study of business models. Although the information we used to create our database was publicly available, we saw that few people had explored the data from a business model perspective and there was still much light to be shed. We were careful to document each step we took, knowing that many people would question the results because of our unconventional thinking and beliefs.

We undertook a wide range of qualitative and quantitative analyses, beginning with traditional metrics, including sales, R&D, return on assets and invested capital, gross margin, and profits. When it was useful, we read analyst reports about each company and examined the words of all the leaders in their quarterly and annual reports to see how they described their own organizations—specifically, whether they were centered on physical assets, services, technology, or networks. Finally, we examined and digested thousands of articles and research by other organizations.

The results of our efforts follow.

Research breakdown

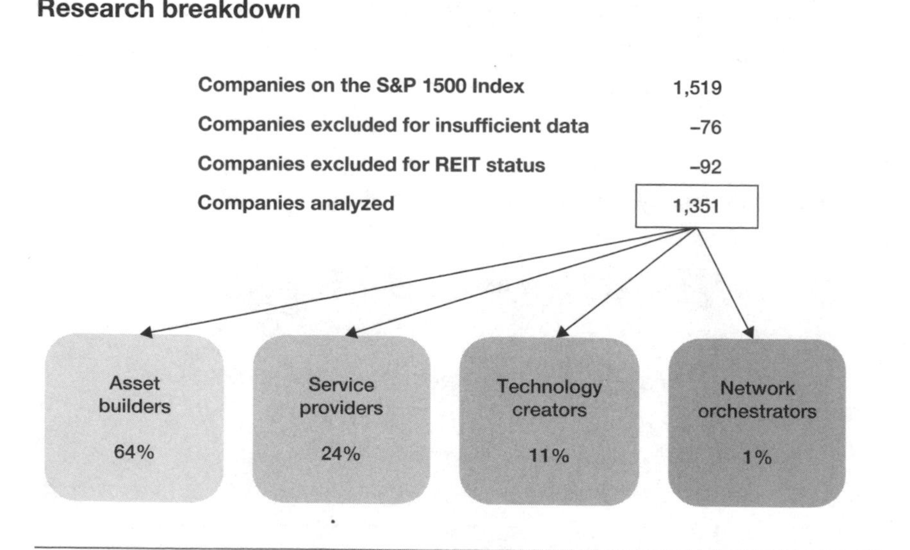

There Are Four Business Models

As we looked into the operations of various firms, we found that nearly all organizations can be classified into one of four *business models*. This term can have many meanings, but here we use it to mean the way that an organization creates value. The four business models that we delineated are as follows.

- *Asset builders* deliver value through the use of physical goods. These companies make, market, distribute, sell, and lease physical things.
- *Service providers* deliver value through skilled people. These companies hire and develop workers who provide services to customers for which they charge.
- *Technology creators* deliver value through ideas. These companies develop and sell intellectual property, such as software, analytics, pharmaceuticals, and biotechnology.
- *Network orchestrators* deliver value through connectivity. These companies create a platform that participants use to interact or transact with the many other members of the network. They may sell products, build relationships, share advice, give reviews, collaborate, and more.

Company examples by business model

Business model	Example companies
Asset builder	Ford, Walmart, Exxon, Boeing
Service provider	Humana, Accenture, JPMorgan Chase
Technology creator	Microsoft, Oracle, Medtronic, Pfizer
Network orchestrator	eBay, Uber, Visa, Red Hat, TripAdvisor

Business Models Are Based on Capital Allocation

Each business model is based on one of four asset types. Asset builders focus on physical capital (things); service providers invest in human capital (people); technology creators develop intellectual capital (ideas); and network orchestrators develop network capital (relationships). The relationships, or connections, created by a network orchestrator may actually provide access to any of the other asset types and leverage a digital platform for connectivity. Here are examples.

- eBay and Etsy are network orchestrators that provide access to physical capital (things you can buy).
- TaskRabbit and Upwork are network orchestrators that provide access to human capital in the form of errand runners and freelancers (people).
- Innocentive and Yelp are network orchestrators that provide access to intellectual capital, such as technological innovation or restaurant reviews (ideas).
- Facebook, LinkedIn, and Match.com are network orchestrators that provide access to network capital, specifically social and professional connections (relationships).

Business Models Scale Differently

When we applied this business model framework to the S&P 1500 (a combination of the S&P large-, mid-, and small-cap indices), it revealed clear and dramatic performance differentials among the four business models. Network orchestrators, on average, grew revenues faster, generated higher profit margins, and used assets more efficiently than companies using the other three business models. These advantages resulted in remarkably higher enterprise values when compared with revenues.

Business model performance

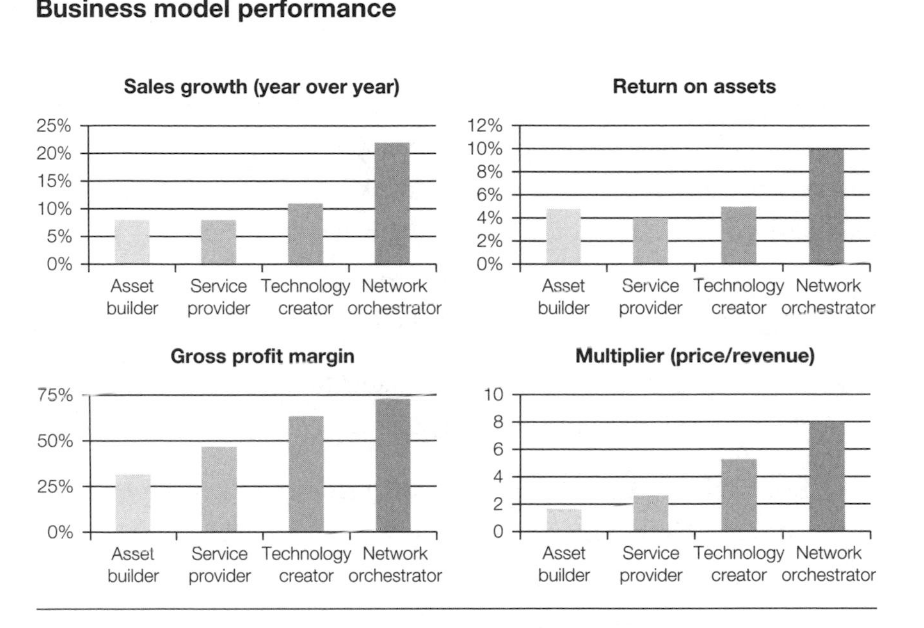

We attribute some of these economic advantages to the ability of digital networks to scale with nearly zero marginal cost (e.g., the cost of each additional good and service made and sold). Digital platforms scale upward very inexpensively compared with other assets. Consider the following.

- To scale up an asset builder, you need additional input materials, plans, and production time in order to build more things.
- To scale up a service provider, you need to recruit, train, and deploy more people.
- To scale up a technology creator is less expensive (for example, selling many copies of software), but it is still not as low cost as a network orchestrator.
- To scale up a network orchestrator is often free; your company need not provide all the value, because the network itself contributes products and content. In fact, network orchestrators rely on their networks to contribute goods, services, information, or relationships to the platform, something that also reduces the burden on the company. This rapid, inexpensive scaling creates favorable profit margins for network orchestrators.

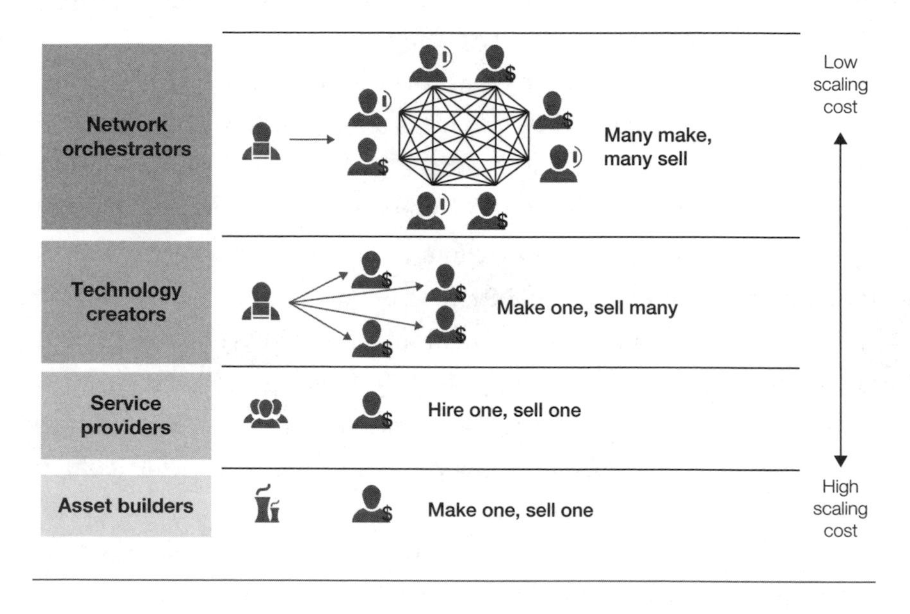

On top of the ease of scaling, network orchestrators benefit from the network's incentive to grow itself. In a network structure (the classic example is a telephone network), the value scales with each additional participant (or node); thus the network participants themselves motivate growth.

Please note that scalability is different than the scale economics that major asset builders have long tried to achieve. Economies of scale are achieved when size, scale of operation, and increased output generally reduce the fixed and variable costs of production and sales. Economies of scale create incremental savings, usually with diminishing returns. Networks scale, on the other hand, exponentially with increasing returns as the number of network participants increases.

Network Orchestrators Are More Valuable

The growth, profit, and scaling advantages of network orchestrators result in unprecedented market valuations. When we examined companies in terms of price (market value) to revenue ratio, which we call a

company's *multiplier*, we found that the average network orchestrator has a multiplier of 8×, compared with 5×, 3×, and 2× for technology creators, service providers, and asset builders, respectively.

To put it simply, this means that if an asset builder earned $100 in revenue, its market value (the total cost of all its stock) would be $200 on average. On the other hand, a network orchestrator with $100 in revenue would have a market value of $800. Said differently, a dollar generated by a network orchestrator is two to four times more valuable to investors than a dollar generated by a traditional asset builder or service provider.

A great market valuation is a useful thing. It increases access to capital and rewards shareholders. Let's not forget, however, what it signifies. Network orchestrators have higher multipliers because the business model is efficient to operate and appealing to the market for its high growth and profit potential. Networks tap in to the excess capacity of assets that previously were unrecognized (for example, the network's professional relationships or its ability to review restaurants) or underutilized (for example, cars and guest bedrooms). In many cases, the cost to access these previously ignored assets is very low.

Business models and multipliers

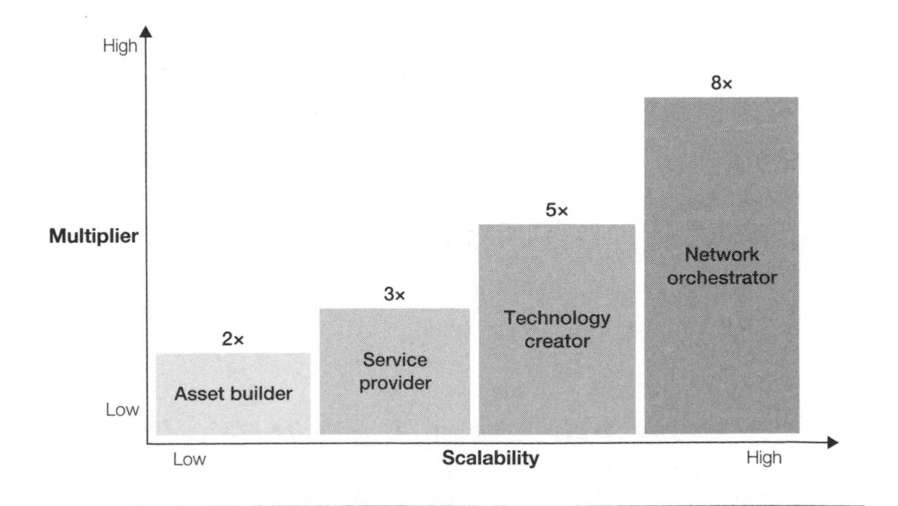

When you enable a network with a digital platform, it can suddenly scale faster and at lower cost than any other type of asset, and digital networks provide users with flexibility, self-service, and autonomy. These advantages are inherent in the form and function of digital platforms, and they're not going away. Why wouldn't you want to be in the part of the market that operates most efficiently and creates the strongest relationships with customers?

Network Orchestrators Create More Value over Time

A high multiplier indicates value at a point in time, but we also wanted to look at value creation over time for different business models. We examined how $1 invested in a portfolio comprised solely of companies using each of the four business models performed over the last ten years. We selected this time period because it covered both bad times (the recession in 2008) and good times (the following growth). Although the network orchestrator portfolio was quite small, since it was a new

Value of $1 invested in business model portfolios in 2005

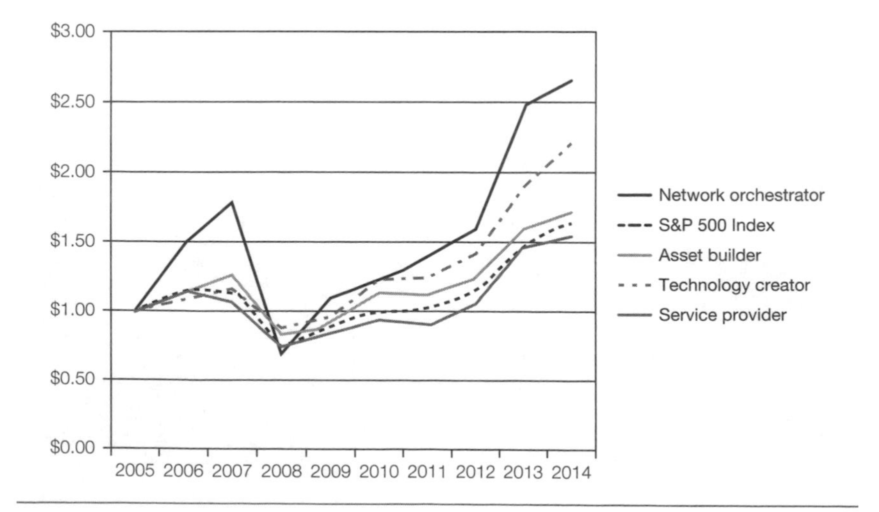

business model, its results were impressive. A dollar invested in a portfolio of network orchestrators outperformed the asset builder portfolio by more than 50 percent.

Interestingly, the S&P 500, which is dominated by large asset-building firms of yesterday, tracked pretty well with asset builders and even service providers. But technology creators (which primarily trade on the NASDAQ) and network orchestrators created significantly higher returns during this time period.

Network Orchestrators Do Things Differently

Your business model, of course, has implications that go far beyond the organizational product line. A business model has implications for all parts of the company, from the assets it invests in, to the way it interacts with customers, to the key performance indicators (KPIs) it tracks. In many regards, network orchestrators operate in ways that run counter to what we're used to thinking of as the best practices of other business models.

If you want to change your business model or augment your organization with highly valuable networks, you need to keep in mind the many dimensions that a business model affects. Based on our observations

Best practices, legacy versus network companies

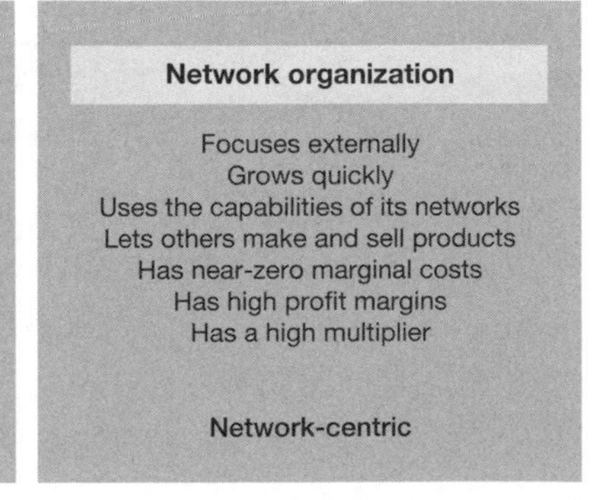
Legacy organization
Focuses internally
Grows slowly
Uses its own capabilities
Sells its own products and services
Has high marginal costs
Has low profit margins
Has a low multiplier
Firm-centric
Network organization
Focuses externally
Grows quickly
Uses the capabilities of its networks
Lets others make and sell products
Has near-zero marginal costs
Has high profit margins
Has a high multiplier
Network-centric

of network orchestrators, we have identified ten principles that describe the ways that these companies are differentiated from their peers using other business models.

Each principle teaches an important lesson and is a lever for creating change, but it is up to you to apply the principles judiciously. The right answer for every firm is not simply to flip wholesale from one extreme to the other, but rather to look at what the network orchestration options offer you—particularly in a network-oriented business—and what makes the most sense given the larger context of your business and your goals.

One of the key factors in network orchestrators is their different thinking. It's easy to think that your organization has been doing business in a particular way for a decade or more, but a network leader has an entirely different mental model. You can, too.

Networks Are Good for Business and for People

Human beings have many wants and needs—from the essentials, like food, shelter, and safety, to the emotional, like esteem and self-expression. Physical networks—highways, aqueducts, electrical grids—are wonderful, but they help us only with our physical needs. As networks have become intangible, or digital, they have gained the ability to serve our deeper needs. Belonging, self-esteem, and self-actualization are *intangible needs* that can be met consistently only through *intangible means.*

For example, Facebook enables us to access and enjoy our friends and family despite the physical distances, not to mention time zone differences, that may separate us. Match.com connects us with romantic partners. LinkedIn broadcasts our professional achievements worldwide. Instagram shares our artistic photography with our friends. Although these connections were possible twenty years ago—for example, via airplanes, matchmakers, headhunters, and art galleries—they were less accessible, more expensive, and much more time-consuming.

Even more important, digital networks are inherently co-creative and user led. Most of us can't help build highways, but all of us can post

pictures of our kids and pets to Facebook. The participants on a network platform contribute the value themselves, whether it is content, art, information, or products. Not only does contributing lead to a sense of ownership and increased affinity, but also it gives the participants outlets to express their desires, mastery, and talents. As members of the network, we self-serve by participating in the platforms that best meet our needs. The network's ability to contribute, and the digital nature of the platform, are what differentiate network orchestrators from networks in the past.

Network Orchestrators Are the Minority

Latent networks exist in and around every organization. However, despite the rapid advancement of digital technology and the remarkable advantages of network business models, very few companies operate as network orchestrators. Our research and analysis of the S&P 1500 found that, in 2014, fewer than 2 percent of the companies used network orchestration as their primary business model. The vast majority still operate as asset builders—making, moving, and selling physical things.

Business models span all industries

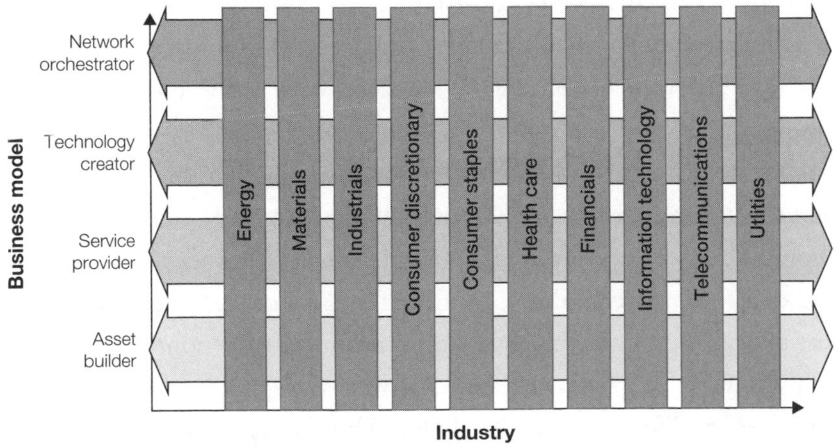

When you consider that asset builders have been around since the Industrial Revolution and that network orchestrators took off only in the past decade, this wildly disparate distribution isn't surprising. But it represents a great market opportunity for legacy firms that are interested in extending their legacies into the future, particularly since business models are industry agnostic and actually span traditional industry verticals. No matter your industry, all business models are available to you. This means that our business model classification doesn't replace, but rather complements, existing industry classifications for understanding a firm's positioning and potential.

The small number of network orchestrators indicates that business leaders are most likely in one of three possible situations.

1. They don't know about or understand network orchestration.
2. They don't believe that the advantages of network orchestration are real or lasting.
3. They don't know how to create network orchestration in their existing business.

This book addresses all three scenarios. If you started in scenarios 1 or 2, lacking information or lacking buy-in, we hope that you have a new lens on the digitally networked world, given the research we've shared in this chapter. The majority of executives we speak with and consult for are in scenario 3—in the know and completely sold on networks, but lost as to real-time, real-people, real-money implementation. They see the rise of exciting network start-ups, note the high valuations given to these organizations, and watch the disruption that is rippling through and across industries. But they don't know how to navigate their own teams and companies successfully through such unfamiliar territory. We aren't the only ones who have noted this.

- Deloitte found that 53 percent of executives see technology enablers or disruptors (or both) on the horizon, companies they consider a threat to their current business model.[1]

- Forrester found that more than 75 percent of executives believe their company does not have the technology, people, processes, or capabilities to execute a reasonable, responsive digital strategy.[2]
- IMD found that only 25 percent of companies are taking a proactive approach to digital disruption.[3]

If you're in this same boat, you're not alone. This book can help. Take the ten principles and the PIVOT process back to your organization, and begin your journey.

There Is Power in the Network

We can all agree that the world is changing. Some have argued that the rate of change is accelerating—and we certainly agree. However, this reality gives us even more reason to seek principles that are universal and timeless despite the changing technology landscape.

Think of it this way: just as the physics of the material world is timeless, so is the nature of being human. We all want to connect with each other, share our experiences, and contribute our skills. We have been doing it since we made cave drawings to pass information from one generation to another. Now we have digital technologies and the networks that are forged on top of them, and our reach is much greater. Leaders who want their organizations to stay relevant and competitive must understand that digital networks are (a) here to stay and (b) gathering money, talent, and market share.

Fortunately for all of us, the scale and profit advantages are inherent in digital technology, and the growth and innovation advantages are inherent in the model. Although it's not simple, it is accessible to you, and it's time to start making forward progress.

THE PRINCIPLES

PART TWO

Ten Strategies for Creating Network Value

AS WE MOVE INTO THE TEN PRINCIPLES FOR NETWORK orchestration, we want to exhort you to consider what each principle has to offer your organization.

Many of these principles will come across as challenges—challenges to your business, your beliefs, and your values. And with challenges often comes resistance. Bringing new thinking to industry incumbents is notoriously hard. Many leaders struggle to see the possibilities, resist letting go of previously successful strategies (even if they are no longer effective), or tinker and tweak without generating any real change.

Instead, try to look at each principle as a lever that could propel you and your organization into a future with greater revenue, profit, growth, and value. You do not need to pull all the levers at once. Some will suit your team and your business immediately, while others might need to be saved for the future. Network orchestration is not one-size-fits-all, and each firm must navigate its own path. But, since the path is unclear, we offer these principles as distinct options to help you make, and track, forward progress on your transformation.

The ten principles are:

1. Create digital capabilities
2. Invest in intangible assets
3. Actively allocate your capital
4. Lead through co-creation
5. Invite your customers to co-create

6. Focus on subscriptions, not transactions

7. Embrace the freelance movement

8. Integrate big data

9. Choose leaders who represent your customers

10. Open your mind to new possibilities

Following each chapter, you can rate your organization on each of the ten principles using the chart on page 122.

These principles are based on themes we have observed in our work with companies of all business models. The principles can be applied individually, but they often apply to the entire organization—which is too much for most leaders to undertake all at once. For this reason, we designed the more detailed PIVOT process, covered in part III, which will help you create network orchestration on a smaller scale.

Remember the power of networks, and create one around you to help guide your company toward a more competitive and profitable future. To start, you could turn to a group of your peers, preferably those with some diversity in their thinking. Ask them to join you on this exciting journey.

PRINCIPLE 1

TECHNOLOGY

From Physical to Digital

The digital revolution is far more significant than
the invention of writing or even printing.

—Douglas Engelbart, internet pioneer

PEOPLE OFTEN HAVE TROUBLE IDENTIFYING WHAT THEY REALLY value, but priorities emerge during times of crisis. In the summer of 2015, waves of Syrians fled the civil war in their homeland. Although the refugees carried food, water, and money in their backpacks, for most of them, the most important survival asset was their smartphone.[1]

When these refugees enter a new country, the first to-do item is to get a new SIM card and get online. This should surprise no one. When combined with internet access, a smartphone can help serve many needs.

Social media and messaging apps keep refugees in touch with family back home and others making the journey. They enable people to share information about the activities of relief agencies and the locations of food, supplies, shelter, and charging stations. Cloud technology helps people access their important information and documents wherever they are. By tracking the best routes between countries via

global positioning, smartphones have even become part of the internet of things.

This story of refugees and their smartphones contains a key message for business leaders: for most of the world, technology is as essential to life as food and water, and it is changing everything. No industry is untouched by the technical revolution, and technology is transforming the back end, the front end, and everything in between—not only manufacturing, not only resource planning, not only marketing and customer relationships, but also the very business models that companies use to create value.

Embrace Digital Everything

There's not much that can't be made better by the addition of digital technology. Think of almost anything you might want to do; there's an app for that. Ten years ago, we were less open with our technology. We welcomed digital into our professional lives in the forms of resource planning, inventory management, word processing, and data crunching, but we kept our personal lives relatively tech-free.

No longer. Now we socialize, decorate our homes, get educated, create art, order dinner, date, adjust the thermostat, exercise, navigate, give to charity, shop, and shop some more, using digital technology—online and, increasingly often, through apps on our personal devices. It's remarkable what we can do with our iPads and what our iPads can do for us, and the day that they begin dispensing Starbucks coffee will truly be grand.

In business, understanding and using digital technology are as important as understanding how profit and loss work. You can't expect to build a great business without it. However, even though many leaders are beginning to incorporate technology piecemeal into various parts of their organizations, few are creating business models that take advantage of digital technology such as social, mobile, cloud, big data analytics, and the internet of things.

Digitally enabled business models offer many advantages to organizations and those they serve. Here are a few of them.

- *Convenience.* When customers are served through digital means, such as online or through an app, they can interact with the organization on their own terms and at their own convenience. The company benefits as well, because it needs fewer physical assets, such as tangible products and property, which depreciate and require maintenance.
- *Access.* Digital products and services scale exponentially and globally quite easily. You can find a doctor or buy a t-shirt from anywhere in the world, with very little added cost or inconvenience. In every industry, we have access to a broader range of options.
- *Integration.* When interaction takes place digitally, it is much easier for the organization to keep records and share information between parties. For example, having a complete online EMR (electronic medical record) reduces the likelihood of errors when you transition between caregivers, are prescribed new medications, or need to see a specialist.
- *Scalability.* A digital platform scales easily to encompass new needs, new providers, and new customers. Airbnb doesn't do much to build out its online platform when hosts or travelers from a new part of the world begin to participate.
- *Analytics.* When customer data, transaction data, and more are stored online, they can more easily be searched, indexed, mined, and analyzed to gain new insights. This offers the opportunity to better serve customers and possibly even create new products from the data itself.

Put simply, digital technology enables you to serve a better product more efficiently. It's a win for businesses and for consumers.

Understand Digital Technologies and Digital Platforms

What do we mean when we talk about *digital technologies?* We know it's based on 0s and 1s, but that's not very helpful. In this book, we usually refer to five key technologies that have had a big impact on customers and organizations.

Mobile technology. Most of us sleep with our smartphones within arm's length. Five billion people use mobile phones and smart devices to interact and transact. This means that more people on Earth have mobile devices than have electricity or drinking water.

Social media. Online platforms allow users to share content such as personal information, text, images, videos, and more in virtual communities. Social media companies develop a platform to connect their communities, but users create most, if not all, of the content. More than one of every five people have an active Facebook account.

Cloud technology. The cloud provides centralized data storage and internet-based access to data, resources, and services. It enables people and businesses to improve utilization of resources, scale rapidly (both up and down), and access data and services through multiple channels and devices.

Big data analytics. This refers to our ability to capture and analyze enormous sets of data, often in real time. Big data helps companies understand their users and themselves and make better decisions.

The internet of things. This web of interconnected, internet-enabled devices lets us collect and use data in order to understand the world, accomplish new tasks, or improve our lives. For example, smart thermostats can learn our daily schedules and make the house toasty warm when we roll out of bed.

Each of these technologies has value in its own right. But when organizations bring digital technology into their business models—the core way they deliver value to customers—their business values start multiplying.

What's a Platform?

Digital platforms are the foundation of the network orchestrator business model. The platform is what enables rapid growth and inexpensive scaling by allowing external parties (the network) to interact with and contribute to the product offering. Platforms often sit on top of, make use of, or are delivered via the technologies just discussed, but what platforms add, in a word, is openness.

In a now (in)famous blog post, Steve Yegge, noted Googler and blogger, ranted about the importance of platforms and explained why Google+ failed to make a dent in Facebook's market dominance of social media.

> A product is useless without a platform, or more precisely and accurately, a platform-less product will always be replaced by an equivalent platform-ized product. . . .
>
> Google+ is a knee-jerk reaction, a study in short-term thinking, predicated on the incorrect notion that Facebook is successful because they built a great product. But that's not why they are successful. Facebook is successful because they built an entire constellation of products by allowing other people to do the work. So Facebook is different for everyone. Some people spend all their time on Mafia Wars. Some spend all their time on Farmville. There are hundreds or maybe thousands of different high-quality time sinks available, so there's something there for everyone.
>
> Our Google+ team took a look at the aftermarket and said: "Gosh, it looks like we need some games. Let's go contract someone to, um, write some games for us." Do you begin to see how incredibly wrong that thinking is now? The problem is that we are trying to predict what people want and deliver it for them.

> You can't do that. Not really. Not reliably. There have been precious few people in the world, over the entire history of computing, who have been able to do it reliably.[2]

Yegge hit the nail on the head. Platforms both permit and invite other people to do the work. Normally, we would call them participants, and people who are participating are far better at determining exactly what they want, when they want it, and how they want it than we are at guessing. What's more, when other parties contribute on your platform, they become partners who have a stake in your success. Digital technology is the underpinning of the platform explosion.

Principle 1, Technology: From Physical to Digital

Physical ▬▬▬▬▬ Digital

Our first principle for becoming a network organization is that you need to move from physical to digital. Digital is the prime mover—the factor that initiated all the changes in business model, culture, and life as we know it. You won't get very far without being digital, but most firms, particularly the biggest ones, are starting with a long legacy of physical assets and thousands of processes, teams, and strategies carefully tuned to the management of those physical assets.

Where does your firm lie on the spectrum from physical to digital? On the left side fall the firms that are grounded in physical goods, such as producers, manufacturers, retailers, and distributors; they have little digital enablement, particularly on the customer-facing side. On the right side are firms with digitally enabled platforms—essentially network orchestrators. In the middle are companies beginning to make the transition to digital by building digital product lines, using big data analytics, and leveraging social media for marketing and communication. Not every firm needs to be on the far right side of the scale, but most need to move significantly in that direction. You may always have physical products in your portfolio, but digital technology can still benefit your firm as well as your customers.

Ask yourself the following questions, and then determine on a scale of 1 to 10 where your company falls in aggregate on the spectrum from physical (1) to digital (10).

(Please note that at the end of part II is a chart where you can note and scale your performance on all ten spectra in one place.)

- Are our core products physical or digital?
- Are we innovators, average users, or laggards in terms of mobile, social, cloud, big data analytics, and the internet of things?
- Do we have the right capabilities (technology, vision, talent) in-house to develop or improve our digital presence?

Don't be discouraged if your mark is far on the left side. You are in good company, with some of the world's oldest, biggest, and best-known firms. But it's time to break away from the pack. If you want to become a digital organization—and the alternative is likely going out of business—you'll need to change.

First, you may need to change the way you, and other leaders in your organization, think about technology. Expunge any sentiment that digital doesn't apply to your organization. It does, inside and out. Second, you need to hire new talent who specialize in digital technologies. This isn't a field where you can train up your existing employees, with old mindsets, in a few months or even years. You need not only new skills but also new ideas. Finally, recognize that both acquiring the talent and building or buying the technology will require capital. Your firm already invests capital each year in assets you find important. It's time to put digital in the mix.

Digital Is a Journey

Adapting to digital technology may seem to be a challenge, but at least it applies to everyone. Even highly digital firms don't get to sit and rest for long. Technology evolves at a lightning pace and, with it, its applications. Even more of our everyday lives is converting to a digital or digitally supported experience.

In March 2014, Facebook purchased virtual reality technology company Oculus VR for $2 billion. According to reports, Facebook founder and CEO Mark Zuckerberg instigated the deal. Zuckerberg described his first time using the VR headset as revelatory: "When you put on the goggles, it's different from anything I have ever experienced in my life."[3] But more than that, Zuckerberg was on the lookout for the next major ecosystem that would support human interaction.

Facebook has already invested a great deal in mobile technology, but he knows it won't be the cutting edge for long: "Strategically we want to start building the next major computing platform that will come after mobile." For the time being, Facebook is letting Oculus manage its own development plan and focus on the video game market, where it began. However, Zuckerberg says, "After games, we're going to make Oculus a platform for many other experiences. Imagine enjoying a courtside seat at a game, studying in a classroom of students and teachers all over the world, or consulting with a doctor face-to-face—just by putting on goggles in your home."

Zuckerberg acknowledges that the technology will evolve, and he wants Facebook to own the platform wherever human beings are interacting. "There are not many things that are candidates to be the next major computing platform," he said. "[This acquisition is a] long-term bet on the future of computing."

Now Is the Time

Since 2000, 52 percent of the *Fortune* 500 companies have been acquired, merged, gone bankrupt, or fallen off the list. It's no coincidence that over that same period, a breakthrough in technology, and the application of that technology to business models, has disrupted industries and set new customer expectations. Moving from physical to digital is now mandatory, and digital platforms are the differentiators for network orchestrators—which, don't forget, benefit from higher revenue growth,

profit margins, and multipliers than companies with other, non-digital, non-platform business models.

Cisco chairman John Chambers predicts that 40 percent of companies will not survive the next ten years, and he says that number is conservative.[4] The only people you will make happy by delaying action on the digital front are your competitors, so consider what you need to commit in time, talent, and capital, and start moving that slider bar from physical to digital.

PRINCIPLE 2

ASSETS

From Tangible to Intangible

The least of things with a meaning is worth more in
life than the greatest of things without it.

—Carl Jung, psychiatrist

IMAGINE SITTING IN YOUR WORK SPACE. LOOK AROUND. WHAT would you say is the most valuable thing in the room?

During the workday, we hope it is you! But we bet that's not what you said.

You may have a Herman Miller chair, fantastic art on the walls, and the latest-generation technology on the desk, but none of these objects is as valuable as a fraction of your time, experience, or expertise. And, great as you are, this situation isn't unique to you. Even someone low on the corporate totem pole has the potential to generate new ideas, connect important people, share experience, and inspire others in ways that objects cannot. Further, although your chair depreciates a little bit every time you sit on it, your value—your ideas, relationships, influence, and capabilities—grows over time with use and experience.

When it comes to the company balance sheet, however, you are an expense, and your chair is an asset.

Let's make another comparison. Which is more valuable—your computer, or the software that runs on it? This is a tougher question, because it is hard to separate the two. If you were to ask your organization's staff accountants, they would probably tell you that a computer is an asset but that much of the software you use is an expense—particularly because a great deal of software is purchased through annual subscription. In the language of accounting, they're right, and even though this doesn't directly answer the question, it is useful information. For any company publicly traded or looking for investors, the classification of assets and expenses matters.

If you took this question to the stock market, however, you would get a different insight. On average, manufacturing companies, such as the one that made your computer, trade at valuations 2× revenues, whereas companies that generate new intellectual capital such as software trade at valuations 5× revenues. Thus, the market values tangible assets and intangible assets differently than corporations and accountants do.

The Sources of Value Are Changing

As recently as 1975, 83 percent of the market value of the S&P 500 companies was made up of tangible assets. In those days, leaders had to focus on plants, inventory, and production. By 2015, however, the proportions had reversed. In 2015, some 84 percent of market value was now composed of intangible assets.[1]

Intangible assets are grounded in people. Things such as our ideas, our relationships, our advocacy, and our experiences are of great value to other people and organizations, and these assets *do not diminish with use*. More often, they appreciate with use. The more time you spend interacting on a social network, the more your influence grows. The more you create and share intellectual capital, the more it improves and the more your credibility grows.

Admittedly, people have always been the source of economic progress. For most of our history, however, our ideas have been focused on the physical—designing new physical products to improve human life or developing new machines and processes to improve productivity. Although we have always instinctually understood intangible assets such as loyalty, experience, and networks, we haven't had the technology to leverage them at scale. Digital technology has made all the difference.

Twenty years ago, your dating pool was limited by the size of your real-life social network. Now, Match.com can introduce you to every registered possible mate in your city. Twenty years ago, an unhappy customer might have been able to hurt your brand with her neighborhood. Now, a terrible customer experience can be tweeted in less than a minute and broadcast around the globe. Twenty years ago, a master carpenter might train a few apprentices in his shop. Now, he can train thousands on a YouTube channel.

Digital technology has vastly increased our individual spheres of influence. Some of this capability still supports the creation, distribution, and use of physical goods, but a great deal of what we choose to put out in the world is the intangible output of our minds—opinions, ideas, preferences, and self-expression.

Let's look at three broad categories you should be aware of when thinking about intangible assets.

PEOPLE AND THE SERVICES THEY PROVIDE. People exist in the physical world, but, despite decades of attempts, people cannot be managed like machines. You cannot turn people on and off like a production plant or move them around for your convenience like inventory. People need to be motivated to do their best work, and motivation is even more complicated with external networks than with employees.

IDEAS AND INFORMATION. Here we refer to the intellectual capital created by people. Software, patents, and biotechnology are common information-based assets, and both the market and traditional accounting systems

are slowly coming up to speed on the management and measurement of valuable ideas.

RELATIONSHIPS AND ACCESS. Human beings are naturally social creatures, and all of us are tied in myriad ways to our familial, social, and professional networks. Within each of these spheres we have different levels and means of influence. Network orchestrators capitalize on the ability of their networks to grow organically as individuals spread the network among those they influence.

Intangible Assets Require New Management Practices

The surge of available intangible assets creates both risk and opportunity for companies. Leaders of digital network organizations realize that success now relies on their ability to manage intangible assets as well as, if not better than, their tangible counterparts. Unfortunately, most corporate leaders have thirty or more years of experience in managing physical assets, and five or fewer years in managing intangible assets. Let's discuss the key differences in modern management, both the good and the bad.

VAST NETWORKS OF INTANGIBLE ASSETS ARE AVAILABLE TO YOU. Digital technology facilitates rapid-fire communication, collaboration, and sharing with those around you. You may have much to learn or much to gain by understanding, and possibly accessing, the intangible assets that lie within your customers, suppliers, distributors, employees, investors, alumni, prospects, and competitors.

CUSTOMERS WIELD GREATER POWER THAN EVER. Properly leveraged, customers can be important assets, touting your brand on Facebook, Instagram, and Twitter, providing valuable product feedback, or even helping you create advertising. On the other hand, ignored, frustrated, or disappointed customers can create a public relations nightmare by sharing video or simply recounting a bad experience on social media.

Comcast made the news in 2014 when a customer, frustrated by a twenty-minute argument about canceling his account, uploaded a recording of the customer service call gone wrong. When it hit the internet, it struck a chord. The clip, uploaded to an audio-sharing service, has been played almost six million times and has received nearly two thousand comments. It was quite a PR nightmare for a company already struggling with image problems.

EMPLOYEES WANT TO CONTRIBUTE DIFFERENTLY. People are becoming more aware of the intangible assets they have to contribute, as well as the value of those assets. This is true in all spheres of life, particularly employment. People want to do far more than execute instructions like classic factory workers. They want to be inspired by a vision and bring their own ideas and talents into play.

A recent study on employee affinity found that 83 percent see recognition of their contributions as more fulfilling than gifts and rewards.[2] Employees also value autonomy and freedom; the freelance economy has grown to 34 percent of the workforce, according to Upwork.[3] This number is expected to balloon to 50 percent within the next five years.[4]

PHYSICAL ASSETS ARE BECOMING FINANCIAL LIABILITIES. With the increased prominence of intangible assets, tangible assets are declining proportionally. Those assets sitting on a balance sheet seem costly to maintain compared with intangibles. The major auto companies, for example, had enormous real estate holdings, many of them factories. Managing and maintaining these holdings drained cash, diluted focus, made the automakers sclerotic, and became a hindrance to innovation. So who then is creating self-driving cars? Why, Apple and Google, of course. These great innovators have few tangible assets relative to their size, and yet they enjoy some of the highest equity values in the world.

Starwood Hotels is another great example. With more than twelve hundred properties under management, Starwood is currently pursuing an asset-light strategy, selling about $1.5 billion in property from 2013 to 2015. The hope is that an asset-light strategy will enable greater

market flexibility and focus on the core business, which is property management and not real estate.

Principle 2, Assets: From Tangible to Intangible

The second principle is to move from tangible to intangible assets. On the left side of the spectrum are companies with physical products, very little intellectual capital, and low use of human capital, either internally or through external networks. On the right side of the spectrum are companies based entirely on intangible assets such as intellectual property or relationships. These companies usually rely on digital technology to support the scaling of their intangible assets.

Those companies on the far right side of the spectrum are network orchestrators that differentiate themselves by accessing the intangible assets of an external network rather than owning and managing assets. Often the assets that they access through their network are wholly intangible. For example, Yelp, Facebook, LinkedIn, TripAdvisor, and Pinterest depend entirely on intangible contributions from the network. Other network companies access the physical assets of the network, such as Uber making use of customers' cars, or Airbnb making use of customers' real estate.

The task of managing external assets, however, is entirely different from managing those owned by your firm. To maintain and grow access to a network's assets, you must carefully manage the sentiment and engagement of the network itself. If Uber doesn't keep its drivers happy, there are other ride-sharing networks such as Lyft and Sidecar ready to take them into the fold.

Let's reflect on your organization and pinpoint where you lie on the spectrum from tangible to intangible. Ask yourself these questions, and then mark on the scale of tangible (1) to intangible (10) where your company falls on the spectrum.

- What are the most important assets of your company? What percentage are tangible? Intangible?
- How much capital and time, by percentage, does your firm allocate to the management of intangible assets?
- How much capital and time, by percentage, does your firm allocate to managing assets that exist outside the firm, such as network assets?
- Is there agreement among the leadership team on which assets are the most valuable?

Most companies fall firmly on the left side of the spectrum. After all, the digital technology that supports the productization and utilization of intangible assets, particularly network assets, has been prevalent only for the past decade. Even so, now is the time to start making a shift.

Don't Learn about the New Assets the Hard Way

Brian Dunn, CEO of Best Buy from 2009 to 2012, was, in his own words, a "store guy." He started as an in-store salesman for Best Buy at the age of twenty-four and worked his way up the ladder. He liked, understood, and excelled at dealing with physical assets.

Dunn's bias for physical assets impacted his actions and therefore how he spent his time and money during his tenure. During the rise of e-commerce, he spent billions of dollars on building new stores and retrofitting older ones, even trying out the big-box format abroad, where it failed miserably.

The investment in stores did have a small upside for customers: Best Buy provided a wonderful opportunity for *show-rooming*, where customers can see and interact with products in person before buying them for lower prices online. Because Best Buy's website, prices, and logistics couldn't compete, it essentially acted as an unpaid auxiliary to

Amazon.com. Meanwhile, Amazon continued to focus on its digital-only storefront and moved into streaming and web services.

It's hard to put too much blame on Dunn. He is in great company with many experienced business leaders who have fallen because of their inability to shift focus and budget away from physical assets. Encyclopedia Britannica was trounced by user-created content on Wikipedia. Kodak failed to act as digital shaped the future of photography. Blockbuster was slain by Netflix.

These companies and their leaders held on to their old mental models past the expiration date. In a rapidly changing environment, the shelf life of mental models is decreasing at an alarmingly fast rate, putting great onus, and pressure, on leaders to keep their thinking fresh and modern.

Shift Your Assets

At one time the *Forbes* 400 wealthiest individuals were primarily railroad barons, but now, half the wealthiest people are technologists. There has been a nearly complete reallocation of value and capital in the market, reflecting a new focus on digital, intangible assets. It is time to take a good look at your asset portfolio and start moving the needle to the right.

PRINCIPLE 3

STRATEGY

From Operator to Allocator

Don't tell me what you value. Show me your budget, and I'll tell you what you value.

—Joe Biden, Vice President of the United States

THE STORY OF IBM IS A CLASSIC OF BUSINESS MODEL INNOVATION. In the 1990s, Lou Gerstner led a company transformation, moving away from a focus on hardware and infrastructure and adding new capability in IT services and consulting. Over Gerstner's tenure, IBM's market capitalization rose from $29 billion to $168 billion.

IBM's journey continues; the market has not stopped moving—it has actually sped up. If it wants to remain a market leader, IBM must continue to shift away from its historical role in manufacturing physical goods and move toward newer digital technologies like big data and the cloud.

When reviewing IBM's evolution over the past few decades for *Forbes*, Bridget van Kralingen, general manager for IBM North America, said simply, "Sometimes companies must fully transform their portfolios."[1] IBM deserves applause for its willingness to reallocate its portfolio.

In 2005, IBM sold its personal-computer business to Lenovo, giving up its stake in an industry it was credited with inventing. Over the past decade, IBM has reallocated much of its capital to investment in high-value, high-growth initiatives, such as the purchase of infrastructure-as-a-service company Softlayer, the development of cloud platform Bluemix, and the creation of an app marketplace. Van Kralingen gives the call to action in crystal clear terms.

> Companies in a crisis need to look at their entire portfolios, rationally and candidly, and figure out what they have that customers want today and what customers will want tomorrow. Then get rid of anything that does not fit the resulting model, and invest in the growth opportunities.
>
> In our case, the information technology industry was rapidly becoming commoditized, and we determined that we needed to shift our portfolio to a more balanced mix of high-value offerings. That meant growing our services and software businesses, both through internal investments and through acquisitions. We have acquired more than 200 companies at a cost of $30 billion to help fill out our portfolio of products and services in these strategic growth areas, such as our growing analytics business.
>
> It also meant divesting low-growth, low-margin product lines and technologies like memory chips, technology components, printers, displays and personal computers. This was easier said than done, as those were technologies, products and even whole markets that we had invented and developed.
>
> In a case like this where a company is struggling to survive, it is easy to understand and accept such change intellectually. It is much harder to grasp it culturally, because of the institutional significance these offerings can have.[2]

This last paragraph emphasizes a key point: this type of change is hard. Institutional memory, historical bias, politics, laziness, and even nostalgia stand in the way of companies that want, or need, to pivot

their business models away from less-valuable assets. Further, leaders don't always think of themselves as asset allocators or think of their businesses as portfolios.

Every Decision Is about Capital Allocation

If you took an introduction to economics course in college, you likely encountered Gregory Mankiw's *Principles of Economics.*[3] This popular textbook opens with ten principles of economics, and the first is this: people face trade-offs. We are always up against a limited supply, whether of money, time, or attention. This is true in our personal lives, and it's true in our professional lives. We don't get to binge-watch TV *and* get in an extra three hours of work in the evening. We can't afford a vacation in Paris *and* in Hong Kong this year. You can't give every division the budget it asks for. Every decision prioritizes one thing over other things.

But we usually don't think of ourselves this way—as allocators of precious resources. Instead, we use tricks to make it less mentally draining to make difficult decisions and assign priorities. We form habits, we do what other people are doing, we give in to the loudest voices, and so on.

But flying on autopilot isn't reliable or advisable if you want to make the best decisions. Have you ever had one of those *aha* moments when you realized you were making bad allocation decisions out of habit? Perhaps you used to mow the lawn every Sunday, grumpily sweating in the summer sun and giving up precious weekend hours, until one day it occurred to you that you could pay someone else to do it. Or maybe it was something else. But we all have moments when we think, "What on earth took me so long to make this change?"

It happens in business, too, and the realization is often too little, too late. Kodak is a great example. In the 1990s, Kodak recognized the imminent transition to digital technology; in fact, it invented the digital camera. But rather than refocus its strategy on the next big thing, Kodak tried to slow the progress of digital technology and maintain

its dominance in film through aggressive advertising. When Kodak finally entered the digital market with its Easy Share product line, it was too late; digital was already on the path to commoditization. In 2012, Kodak filed for Chapter 11 bankruptcy.

These situations happen because our mental models prevent us from seeing the need for change and, even when we see it, from acting on it. IBM probably could not have shed its PC business—once a jewel in its portfolio, representing innovation and daring, the ability to rapidly innovate, and an exciting success over Apple—if Sam Palmisano had not just come into the CEO role with a mandate to focus on high-margin, high-growth businesses. With this new perspective, Palmisano was able to push through the controversial sale to Lenovo in order to reallocate IBM's time, talent, and money to more-fruitful ground.

Companies Are the Biggest Capital Allocators

If asked to describe themselves, most leaders of organizations would likely say they're business operators rather than capital allocators. So you might be surprised to learn that companies with multiple businesses allocate about $640 billion annually, even more than capital markets allocate.[4]

What do corporations do with that $640 billion? Probably the same thing they did last year. McKinsey found that the average correlation between one year's allocation and the previous year's was 0.92 (a correlation of 1 is a perfect match). For one-third of companies, the capital allocation was almost exactly the same as the previous year—a 0.99 correlation.[5]

It's astounding. A lot can change in a year. Externally, your industry may see new entrants, new technologies, and new customer preferences. Internally, you learn about business model performance, the capabilities of new leaders, and the performance of new assets. But despite all that new information, asset allocation changes very little year to year.

If that sounds like a problem to you, you're right. It makes little sense, given new information, to do the same old thing, but that's what most

of us do. The same McKinsey study found that the most active reallocators, regardless of sector, delivered returns to shareholders 30 percent higher than the least active reallocators. And CEOs who reallocated less actively in the first three years of their term were more likely than their active peers to lose their position in years four through six. It makes a compelling case.

Principle 3, Strategy: From Operator to Allocator

Operator → Allocator

The third principle we teach is to move from operator to allocator. On the left side of the spectrum, the leadership team focuses on operating the business effectively but doesn't actively use the lever of reallocation to shift time, talent, or capital to adapt the company's strategy and business model in real time. These companies usually keep doing what they've been doing, with the goal of improving gradually over time. For example, an automaker whose leaders are operators will build increasingly better cars. In contrast, an automaker whose leaders are allocators—another word might be *investors*—might shift its business model from automaker to transportation facilitator over some years through strategic reallocation.

Note that companies still need good operators to run a business well. But those operators need to be focused on the right business model, and that's why capital allocation is essential.

Acting like an allocator doesn't necessarily mean that you will automatically be a network orchestrator, but you won't be able to shift your asset allocation, and therefore your business model, without taking on an investor mentality. Further, maintaining an investment or allocation mindset will help you stay current, no matter where technology or business models go in the future.

Consider your own organization, and your leadership team, and determine where you fall on the spectrum from operator to allocator.

Ponder the following questions and mark on the scale where your team falls from operator (1) to allocator (10).

- Does your organization react to annual budgeting as a chore to be completed, or as an opportunity to create a brilliant future?
- Do you begin the budgeting process with a draft of last year's budget? How far do you move from it? Or do you instead use a zero-based budgeting process?
- What factors influence your team to be conservative on reallocation? Fear? Politics? Time constraints? Market pressure?
- Does your team have the capability, skills, and insights needed to keep up with market shifts and potential alternative investments?

As McKinsey's research indicates, most companies fall on the left side of the spectrum, but you have the opportunity every day to actively reallocate by making new decisions.

What Do the Best Allocators Do?

From our experience working with leaders and organizations, we've observed some best practices that active allocators use to keep their capital allocation fresh. Here's what we recommend.

SET ALLOCATION GOALS. We're sure that your organization has many goals, and often specific and measurable ones. But do you have targets for capital allocation? Has your leadership team agreed that a certain percentage should be spent in high-growth, transformational areas? We recommend 10 to 20 percent to begin a business model transformation.

MAKE PRUNING A PART OF YOUR PROCESS. The hard part isn't saying yes; it's saying no. In any pool of assets, there are usually a few laggards or underperformers. Selling or closing these projects will clear space

for more-valuable ones. Create guidelines that will help you commit to making difficult decisions, such as the goal of eliminating the bottom 10 percent of performers.

USE DIFFERENT ANCHORS. It's easy and understandable to use last year's budget as a starting point, but doing so anchors your teams to these numbers and makes active reallocation much more difficult. Courageous zero-based budgeting helps, but you can also use another approach to help shake up perspectives. For example, you could review what the budget would be if it were allocated based on percentage of revenue generated. Or on last year's growth. Or on expected growth. Or on customer satisfaction. We don't recommend making a budget based on any of these alone, but together these data points can help the team see perspectives other than last year's numbers.

SET THE EXAMPLE. Keep in mind that as a leader you set the example for your peers and teams. You're not going to hold hands down the chain and review each allocation, so you want to demonstrate the right behavior for everyone else. Use this as motivation when the going gets tough.

A Little Inspiration

Starbucks and Nike have tangible, non-digital core products: coffee and sneakers, respectively. They're asset builders, and, based on our analysis, we would expect them to have price-to-revenue ratios in the 2× range. Instead, as of this writing, Nike was at 3.26, and Starbucks sat at 4.80. Those are strong numbers for thing-based companies.

The two companies' higher market values are driven by their willingness to innovate and invest beyond their historical business models. Nike has partnered with Apple, developed hardware and software, and expanded its social media presence with the Nike+ ecosystem. Starbucks has developed a wildly popular app that is now a mobile payment system.

It took guts to invest the time, talent, and technology to make these initiatives, but there is a reason these companies are market leaders.

They haven't achieved the 8× multipliers of network orchestrators (yet), but that is because only a fraction of their businesses is in the more valuable business model. But that fraction affects the value and trajectory of the entire company. Moreover, it differentiates them in the market and has the potential to grow into new core businesses.

Just as in our personal financial portfolios, it's smart to diversify as a buffer against risk. Of course, it's risky to take your organization outside historical areas of expertise. It's also risky, as Blockbuster and Kodak have eloquently proven, to remain in your historical areas of expertise when their value is diminishing.

Challenge yourself and your team to *allocate* with the same focus that you *operate*, and create a business with greater profit, growth, and value.

PRINCIPLE 4

LEADERSHIP

From Commander to Co-creator

A leader's job is not to do the work for others, it's to help others figure out how to do it themselves, to get things done, and to succeed beyond what they thought possible.

—Simon Sinek, author, *Start with Why*

IN 2003, GENERAL STANLEY MCCHRYSTAL TOOK COMMAND OF THE Joint Special Operations Task Force. What began as a military campaign against the Saddam Hussein regime eventually evolved into a prolonged, complex, and chaotic fight with Al-Qaeda in Iraq. For several years, the fight did not go well.

The task force had highly capable and experienced leaders, extremely disciplined soldiers, and the best technology and communications equipment money could buy. Al-Qaeda in Iraq had untrained fighters, had to deliver messages by courier, and used improvised, outdated weaponry. And yet the number of insurgent attacks was still increasing, not decreasing.

What McChrystal found, as documented in his book *Team of Teams: New Rules of Engagement for a Complex World*, is that the old ways of leading and structuring no longer matched the digital, deeply

interconnected world.[1] Old habits and old mental models needed to be updated, or discarded, to combat an enemy that lived and recruited online, had no permanent barracks or hierarchy, and changed identity as easily as it changed clothes.

So McChrystal altered the structure of the task force, and then the whole team changed its way of managing it. As he describes the transformation, "We reworked many of the precepts that had helped establish our efficacy in the twentieth century, because the twenty-first century is a different game with different rules."[2]

They broke down the walls and hierarchies of the organization and remade them around new principles that reinforced adaptability and agility: trust, common purpose, transparent information sharing, and decentralized decision-making authority. They found that this organization was far more effective in dealing with the target.

As you would imagine, leading this new organization was an entirely different task. It required "transparent leadership that empower[ed] team members" and a refocus on creating an environment where everyone could and would perform to the best of their ability rather than being micromanaged. In short, McChrystal and his team needed to shift from commanding to co-creating.

This is the type of leadership that network orchestration requires. We don't want you to think about business as battle. That would be antithetical to our purpose. But we do want you to think about leadership as a two-way street. It is a role that requires collaboration, facilitation, and co-creation rather than merely direction and control.

Relationships Are Changing

People are relating to the world differently from the way they used to, and that means leaders must relate to their worlds differently. Historically, for the most part, our relationships used to be based on family and proximity. We communicated in person or through the written word, and our sphere of influence was limited. We were similarly limited in

our work and our contribution. We shared the products of our hands or minds with those we could physically reach.

Now we can form relationships with anyone in the world. We communicate through pictures, videos, links, likes, and shares as much as actual conversation. And each of us has a sphere of influence that is limitless, provided we can pay enough money or say something interesting enough. All this affects the way we act and interact socially, at work, and as consumers. We cover these topics in more detail later in the book. For now, let's look at an overview.

WE HAVE MORE OPTIONS. Digital technology puts the world at our fingertips. We can find friends and affinities as easily with people across the world as we can with our own neighbors. We can buy any one of twenty-five hundred blenders through Amazon.com. We can work virtually for employers around the world.

If your employees or customers aren't happy with you, they can jump ship in less than a heartbeat. Deloitte has found that customer loyalty to brands has declined steadily since 2010.[3] What's more, the American Management Association found that leadership teams view their employees as less loyal than they used to be.[4]

WE HAVE MORE INFORMATION. The amount of information we can access is astonishing, and its quality is markedly improved and improving. Not only can we buy twenty-five hundred different blenders on Amazon.com, but also we can see thousands of reviews for those blenders. When considering career moves, we can look at the salaries of workers across industries and companies to figure out where we want to go next. And when a company experiences a public relations nightmare in the form of a political misstep, environmental accident, or customer service disaster, we can see that, too.

Combining information with options is powerful. Further, given that organizations have the same or even better access to predictive analytics, they can increasingly send us relevant information in real time,

thereby effectively increasing our options. Now when we hear something displeasing about an organization, we can easily vote with our pocketbooks (and clicks) for the next competitor.

WE LIKE TO PARTICIPATE. Social media allows us to interact with organizations in a direct and personal way—for example, tweeting at the CEO. Network orchestration allows us to participate directly in value creation—for example, posting a back bedroom on Airbnb. We want the same type of access and ownership as employees. Rather than cogs in a machine, we want to be valued partners.

These types of interactions make us feel an intimate and personal connection with companies. The brands that we tout on Facebook become a part of our own brand. The companies that we work with, either as employees or as network participants, also become part of our livelihood. This relationship increases our potential loyalty but also raises the stakes, because we don't want to share our brand and our work with just anyone.

These three factors—more options, more information, and more participation—change us as employees and as customers. They also mandate a change in leadership style. The network orchestration business model requires that leaders interact with their employees and their customers on a whole new level. Motivating customers to buy is different from motivating them to contribute. Telling an employee to do something is different from giving her the tools and space to figure out how she should do her job. Changes in both culture and business mean that communication, inspiration, and facilitation are bigger parts of the job than ever.

A New Environment Requires New Leadership Styles

As McChrystal put it, "The role of the leader becomes creating the broader environment instead of command-and-control micromanaging." The leader of an asset-building organization needs to manage plants, watch inventory and costs, and convince the customer to buy.

The leader of a network-orchestrating company may do those things as well, but he also must set up an environment where his networks are enabled to contribute as partners, and then motivate members of those networks to co-create with the organization. Where the old style of leader is a commander, the new style of leader is a co-creator.

What's tricky is that co-creation requires you to give up control—at least, some control.

When you partner with others, whether they're employees, customers, suppliers, or investors, they will likely bring something unexpected to the table, and it will probably cause you to adjust your grand vision. If you're in commander mode, that will look and feel threatening. If you're in co-creator mode, it will look and feel intriguing. It all depends on your mental model, which influences your business model and your leadership style.

When Jack Dorsey and his collaborators developed Twitter in 2006, employees of the start-up used it internally. Cofounder Evan Williams described what happened.

> There was this path of discovery with something like that, where over time you figure out what it is. Twitter actually changed from what we thought it was in the beginning, which we described as status updates and a social utility. It is that, in part, but the insight we eventually came to was Twitter was really more of an information network than it is a social network.[5]

Dorsey and his partners had no idea of the role Twitter would play in sociopolitical movements, pop culture, and business until the network actually started forming. Although it's natural for any inventor or operator to resist others shaping her creation or carefully managed domain, this is the path to greatest value, for who knows better than the users how they can use the tool to greatest advantage?

And don't be deceived. As a leader, the co-creator is just as active and important as the commander; the actions are simply different. Whereas a commander needs to figure out everything independently so that it can be communicated downward, the co-creator facilitates an ecosystem where the network figures itself out, and then the network

communicates upward to ask for what it needs. The commander knows and instructs; the co-creator listens and synthesizes.

Principle 4, Leadership: From Commander to Co-creator

Commander ▬▬▬▬ Co-creator

The fourth principle is to move from commander to co-creator. On the left side of the spectrum are leaders who prefer a structured, hierarchical, top-down organization and count on themselves to create and communicate the strategy. On the right side of the spectrum are leaders who seek insight outside themselves and who know how to motivate and inspire those around them to collaborate in building something together.

It is impossible to lead a company with a network orchestrator business model if you're acting like a commander all the time. Network orchestration requires the active, eager, engaged participation of "assets" that you don't own and that don't report to you. People won't contribute to your network if they feel you're using them as tools rather than as valued and respected partners. Here are some of the ways that co-creators care for and engage their networks.

THEY MAKE THEMSELVES ACCESSIBLE. Co-creators understand that the best ideas and insights come from a hugely diverse group of stakeholders. Internally, they make themselves accessible to employees, regularly take comments and questions, and facilitate the momentum of innovative ideas—for example, through an idea "stock exchange" where the top performers get funding.

Externally, co-creators engage with their networks whenever possible and through all available channels—from in-person to Facebook to Twitter to Instagram and wherever else the network is making its presence felt. Co-creators know exactly what is being said about their products and service offerings on Yelp, Angie's List, and Amazon.com.

THEY PUSH DECISIONS DOWNWARD. Co-creators recognize that they cannot make all the decisions. Further, they often are not the right persons to make the decisions, even if they could. Many decisions can be made best by the people closest to the effect the decisions will have; for example, Airbnb's team does not decide what types of properties or what cities will be added to the network. The network makes those decisions.

Enabling appropriate decision making at all levels inside and outside the organization also shows respect for members of the network and encourages both their self-determination and their ability to self-serve.

THEY CREATE SHARED VISION AND VALUE. Co-creators co-design, truly believe in, and facilitate a vision for their organization that everyone buys in to and everyone profits from. The keyword is *everyone*; this means no exceptions. Every single person who touches and is touched by a co-creatively led organization is connected to its explicitly stated purpose.

The corporate culture must reflect the vision as well. One of the keys to network orchestration is making sure that members of the network receive value commensurate with or greater than that of their participation. That value is sometimes monetary, but it can also be the satisfaction or esteem that comes from participating in the creation of something inspiring.

You may not use your co-creative style all the time, but consider how capable you are when you use it. To what degree do you follow each of the actions just described? Mark where you fall on the spectrum from commander (1) to co-creator (10). Have your whole team do the same.

Leaders Are Still Unique Individuals

No two leaders are alike, and neither are two co-creators. In this discussion of leadership style, it's important to remember that we're focused not on personality characteristics, but on actions. Making yourself

accessible, pushing decisions downward, and creating a shared vision are actions that you can take regardless of your personal nature. You don't need to be warm and fuzzy like a teddy bear in order to motivate co-creation, although we wouldn't rule it out.

Nor do you need to be a co-creator in every circumstance. Just as companies are portfolios of assets, leaders need to have access to and employ a portfolio of styles. Let's take a look at how this played out for one great leader.

Steve Jobs isn't often remembered for his co-creative leadership style. He is more often remembered for his difficult personality, emotional outbursts, and perfectionism. When Jobs had a clear vision for a product, he was notoriously dogmatic about enforcing it. However, he also created open Apple platforms and drew in a developer network that earned $10 billion in 2014.

Jobs had more than 450 patents and helped design multiple market-creating products, but when asked by his biographer, Walter Isaacson, about his greatest accomplishment, he said, "You know, making a product is hard, but making a team that can continually make products is even harder. The product I'm most proud of is Apple and the team I built at Apple."[6]

Co-creation may not yet be the most comfortable style for many leaders, just as it wasn't for Jobs, but it is simply required if you want to tap in to the value of network orchestration. Relinquishing control and sharing value are the only ways to motivate the needed participation and sharing from the network that forms the core of the network orchestrator business model. Remember the 8× price/revenue multiplier earned by network orchestrators, and keep letting go and empowering your networks.

Co-creation Leads to Value

In the end, the argument for leaders to co-create is an argument for profit, growth, and value. Network orchestration taps in to the assets, skills, insights, and relationships of groups external to your firm. The

external network enables low or near-zero marginal cost of scaling as well as rapid growth, higher profit margins, and, ultimately, greater investor returns. But to get there requires many leaders to take on a new set of skills.

Every one of us possesses a portfolio of leadership styles, and each one has its place. A surgeon may be a commander in the operating room, and a co-creator when developing a treatment plan. Find your inner co-creator and start increasing value creation—for customers, employees, and investors.

PRINCIPLE 5

CUSTOMERS

From Customers to Contributors

> What makes eBay successful—the real value and the real power
> at eBay—is the community.
> It's the buyers and sellers coming together
> and forming a marketplace.
>
> **—Pierre Omidyar, founder, eBay**

EVERY COMPANY WANTS TO INCREASE ITS CUSTOMERS' LIFETIME value and share of wallet. Often, the first step is to measure loyalty. A loyal customer is likely to be a repeat buyer with lower acquisition costs. Perhaps fifteen years ago, companies became sophisticated in their understanding of customer value and began looking at advocacy or promotion. In 2003, Fred Reichheld of Bain & Company introduced the popular Net Promoter Score (NPS), which measures the likelihood of your customer base to recommend your products or services to friends and family.

In the intervening years, company focus on customer advocates has grown. The firms with which customers frequently interact request or

incentivize their likes on Facebook and their tweets on Twitter. They give us coupon codes to share with our friends and family and send us branded swag so that we can advertise for them while on the go. To sum up, at first companies wanted only our money—and hoped to get it again and again. Then they wanted our voices, which can be used to promote the brands we love with much more credibility than paid advertising.

Now it goes even further. The most valuable customers are the ones who provide companies not only their money, not only their voices and promotion to others, but also their ideas, insights, services, assets, and relationships. These are the customers that we call contributors. *Customer contributors* act as an extension of the organization itself and may take on any role, including designers, producers, content creators, salespeople, and price setters. In exchange for value they receive, they contribute real value to the operations of the firm. But this is not the money-for-products relationship to which we have become accustomed. Instead it is ideas-for-esteem (Yelp), assets-for-revenue (Airbnb and Uber), or any of a number of nonstandard agreements between companies and customers.

Companies that tap in to the contributions of their customer networks are most successful when the relationship is fulfilling and rewarding to customers. On the fulfillment side, winners seek ways that their customers can contribute that the customer will enjoy. On the reward side, the best-performing organizations return fair compensation for the network's insights and contributions; remember that this partnership must be mutually beneficial.

We buy products and services every day. But ask yourself how many of those products you have helped design. How many products or services have your mark on them? Is it 1 percent, 5 percent, maybe 10 percent? When there are many ways for companies to interact with their customers, why is it that few companies really allow you to co-create with them on products and services? After all, don't you know what your wants and needs are? Just check your iPhone, and see all the modifications you have made to it. Despite enormous potential, few companies truly tap in to the contributive potential of their customer networks.

Lego Makes the Most of Its Fans

In 2004 things had gone off the rails at family-owned Danish company Lego Group. Revenues were down, debt was up, and the trend was not positive. Founded in 1932 by Ole Kirk Christiansen, a carpenter, Lego had an ambitious, inspiring mission: "Our ultimate purpose is to inspire and develop children to think creatively, reason systematically and release their potential to shape their own future—experiencing the endless human possibility."[1]

But missions can be fulfilled only by companies that are still operating. In 2004, Jørgen Vig Knudstorp took on the role of CEO—the first nonfamily member to lead the company—and began a great turnaround. Returning the company to profitability was the obvious goal, and it required a cultural shift. Historically, Lego employees focused more on doing good and nurturing children, and less on meeting deadlines, budgets, and goals. Knudstorp had to change this attitude—and he did.

Now you might think that Lego's return to profitability required it to focus inward, putting efficiency and operations ahead of customer wants, and it's true that understanding product line profitability and cutting SKUs was a part of its success. But a huge element of Lego's success under Knudstorp has been in looking outward to better leverage customers. Knudstorp put it this way:

> The Lego community, like the basic interchangeable plastic brick, is one of the company's core assets. I think I realized the power of customer contributions in 2005, when the company started involving a couple of enthusiastic fans in product development and I started systematically meeting with adult fans of Lego. Since then, we've actively encouraged our fans to interact with us and suggest product ideas. An amazing number of grown-ups like to play with Legos. While we have 120 staff designers, we potentially have probably 120,000 volunteer designers we can access outside the company to help us invent.[2]

Although Lego owns a fairly small niche in the toy market, its brand awareness and customer affinity are phenomenal. Over the past decade, Lego has engaged its customers so thoroughly that they are almost a part of the company itself. On the Lego Ideas web page, customers share their ideas for new Lego sets. Ideas that gather ten thousand supporters go before a review board, which selects the best options, and those aligned with Lego's values, for production. The latest release from Lego Ideas is the lovable robot from Pixar's movie *WALL-E.*

Lego also facilitates interaction among customers, helping Lego enthusiasts of all ages share their passion and great ideas. Lego has a thriving community of enthusiasts who share words, photos, and videos. The Lego Digital Designer software, which customers can use to create and share their own custom designs (along with instructions for building them), is available free. Knudstorp even hired AFOLs (adult fans of Legos) as designers.

Lego has now returned to profitability and has gained great success for creating products that its customers truly love. In February 2015—following the success of *The LEGO Movie,* which emphasized the role of customers as contributors—Brand Finance, an intangible asset valuation consultancy, rated Lego's brand as the most powerful in the world.[3]

The Value of Contribution

Customer contribution and co-creation bring enormous value to companies that utilize them, across a wide range of industries. To examine these sources of value, let's take a closer look at one of the most co-creative companies out there: the t-shirt company Threadless. Founded in 2000 by Jake Nickell and Jacob DeHart, Threadless began as an outlet for freelance graphic designers. Each week, the Threadless community, more than two million strong, submits and votes on thousands of designs. Anyone, pro or novice, can submit a design. The best and most popular are then printed in limited editions and sold to a waiting audience. The artists receive a share of the revenues of their product.

Threadless recognizes that the online community is its most valuable asset, so let's look at the myriad ways the company benefits from this network.

Talent. Threadless is an innovative apparel design company, with no designers on staff. Their artists are an external community, motivated largely by the goal of seeing their artwork out in the world. Threadless does not need to find, recruit, or train these artists, nor does it need to worry about keeping their skills up-to-date.

Insight. Threadless never faces the problem of an unpopular product. It prints only the t-shirt designs that the community loves and votes for. The system automatically keeps the company up-to-date on the latest trends. Further, based on the number of voters for each design, Threadless has great insight into expected sales numbers and even size and color distribution.

Agility. Have tastes changed? No problem. When nautical themes go out of style and outdoorsy images come in, Threadless is ready to go. The external artist network has its finger on the pulse of style, and the voting system fine-tunes the product line to current tastes. The system automatically adapts to change.

Scalability. Because the talent is external and the voting infrastructure is online, Threadless can easily scale up or down the number of designs it selects or the number of shirts it prints. Fixed costs are minimal. Further, because of the data the company receives weekly through the voting system, it knows immediately when a change of scale is required.

Access. Through its network of artists, Threadless has access to all of their respective networks. This is true of any group of potential "promoters" for an organization, but in this case, the network has a lot more incentive. Because the artists become co-creative partners, when they promote Threadless, they also

promote themselves. The artist network is essentially an extended marketing and sales team.

Affinity. Last, but most important, contribution and co-creation build a deep and mutual relationship between customers and the firm. These relationships are self-reinforcing and build a sense of "we are all in this together." Great affinity magnifies all the other benefits that a network can provide. You may like a company that sells great products, but you are more likely to love a company that treats you like an asset and shares value with you.

Although this is an extensive list of benefits, don't feel that you need to check every box from the beginning. Threadless and Lego use customer contribution via their respective networks in unique ways that best fit their businesses and their customer bases, and you can, too. Contribution is just as valuable on a small scale: Nike ID, for example, allows you to customize your own pair of sneakers by choosing colors, patterns, and materials. You can even put your name on the back—your own personal brand. Try asking for that next time you spend $60,000 on a luxury car—customizing your car with your name rather than the maker's.

Why Do You Need Customer Contribution Now?

Given that customer contribution is a valuable tool for businesses, why have we seen it take off only in the past decade? It's the technology, of course. Digital technology enables new ways of interacting with, learning from, and catering to customers.

Both Threadless and Lego use online forums to gather data from their customers on the products they want to see next. Uber uses mobile technology and big data to locate drivers and price services. Nike uses the latest manufacturing technology to produce shoes cost-effectively in batches of one.

Most of these technologies were not available twenty years ago. But they are now—and savvy companies are making good use of them.

Principle 5, Customers: From Customers to Contributors

Customers ——— Contributors

As you can probably tell, the fifth principle is to move your customers to contributors. On the left end of the spectrum lie companies that value their customers primarily for the money in their wallets. Transactions and loyalty, leading to future transactions, are the goals of these firms. As you move to the right side of the spectrum, you broaden the customer value added, first by incorporating their voices as promoters and then by including their tangible and intangible assets as well. The firms that best utilize contributors interact with their customers as complete human beings, understanding not only what they want but also what they want to contribute—whether ideas, reactions, services, products, assets, or their personal networks.

Note that this principle pairs nicely with principle 4: commander to co-creator. As leaders become co-creators, they partner with other people who want to contribute their ideas and skills. You can't co-create by yourself, after all. Contributions can come from any external network (not only customers), including suppliers, distributors, investors, communities, alumni, and even competitors. We've focused on customer networks in this chapter because everyone has them and most are underutilized, and because increasing affinity with customers has the highest payout.

As discussed previously, not every company will go to a business model that is 100 percent dependent on customer contribution, but there are significant gains to be made by even small steps. Here are some of the actions that companies often take in the early stages of developing contributive relationships with customers.

Engage your superusers. Every organization has a group of customers who know the products better than the sales team or love them better than the designers. This group will be the most eager

to contribute to the firm and also is likely to have insight into where its contributions can bring the most value.

Give options. At the beginning of this journey, it's hard to know exactly which network, which channel, and which topics will create the best contribution channel. Provide flexible options at first, and then invest iteratively in what is working. These options do not have to be expensive or complicated; for example, the Threadless concept started on a discussion forum. You can also use Facebook, YouTube, and Twitter.

Listen a lot. The goal is to receive something of value from your customers, and the first piece will certainly be insight on how to better engage them for contribution. Plan to spend a lot of time listening at the beginning so that you can adapt effectively.

Give back. Remember that customers will contribute only as a part of a two-way, beneficial relationship. The network participants who spend their time, energy, and assets with your organization should receive commensurate value in return. Think carefully about how to show them your respect and appreciation in ways that matter to them. If you don't know how, ask them.

How far has your organization gone to build a mutual relationship with your customers and turn them from passive receivers of products and services into contributors who partner with your firm? Consider where your organization falls between customers (1) and contributors (10).

Customer Contribution Is for Companies Big and Small

We've talked a lot about Threadless and Lego, but don't make the mistake of thinking that customer contribution is only for start-ups, small firms, or those that sell consumer goods. Any firm of any size can benefit from customer contribution.

Consumer food giant General Mills launched its own network, the General Mills Worldwide Innovation Network. On G-WIN, budding inventors and collaborators can suggest innovations in six areas: products, packaging, processes, ingredients, technologies, and digital. In 2014, twenty-four-year-old Mark King responded to a request on G-WIN for a new method to assess the texture (crunchy or chewy) of granola bars. General Mills was excited to collaborate with King on the design of the new machine and is currently pursuing a patent.

Several other major firms, including Eli Lilly and Company, NASA, AstraZeneca, and the *Economist*, leverage the online platform Innocentive for external contributions. A network orchestrator itself, Innocentive facilitates organizations to tap in to a broad network of problem solvers to create new ideas and solve difficult problems "faster, more cost effectively, and with less risk than ever before."[4] Innocentive solvers have found new ways to clean up oil spills, have discovered biomarkers for diseases, and have simplified the manufacturing processes for pharmaceuticals.

The Network Is a Resource

What Threadless, eBay, Lego, and many others have realized is that their networks of customers are remarkably valuable resources, not only for the money they spend on products but also for their advocacy, insight, talent, and assets. Naturally, not all of your customers will want to contribute to your firm, and this is fine. But some portion of them will be eager to engage. There will always be more people and resources external to your company than within it—and why wouldn't you want to access and use these resources? Turn your gaze outward, and leverage your most essential network: your customers.

PRINCIPLE 6

REVENUES

From Transaction to Subscription

In a transactional business, the person
really is probably only going to
come around once or maybe twice
if you have a really high repeat order rate.
But in a subscription business, you're
going to see them by definition,
over and over and over and over again.
And you're going to have an opportunity to impress them
every single time. You're in a relationship.

—John Warrillow, author, *The Automatic Customer*

DO YOU BOX? WE DON'T MEAN THE SPORT WITH THE BIG GLOVES. We're talking about participation in a new business phenomenon: at a regular cadence, boxes full of carefully selected, novel, and delightful goods appear on your doorstep as if it's Christmas morning.

The subscription-box industry has exploded in the past few years. Birchbox was one of the first and best-known curated box companies. Founded by Harvard Business School grads Katia Beauchamp and

Hayley Barna, Birchbox delivers to its customers' doorsteps each month a set of selected samples of high-end beauty products. Birchbox now has more than 800,000 subscribers, has diversified into e-commerce and brick-and-mortar, and is valued at $485 million.

If perfumes and makeup aren't your thing, fear not. There is a box for you. Perhaps you'd like to indulge your beloved dog with a BarkBox full of treats and toys. Or maybe you'd like a palate refresher with a regular delivery of new wine (Club W), tea (Tea Sparrow), or coffee (MistoBox). If you're tired of grocery shopping, Blue Apron will deliver fresh ingredients and recipes for three dinners each week. You can keep the kids busy with crafts and activities from a Kiwi Crate, a Koala Crate, or a Groovy Lab in a Box, among many others. Need some thank-you cards to send for all those boxes? Nicely Noted will send you beautiful Letterpress cards and stamps each month. Fishing lures? Socks? Razors? Art? Vitamins? There's a box for that.

And subscription boxes aren't just for start-ups. Large, established businesses can also see the benefits of boxes: product exposure, regular touch points with customers, and recurring revenue models. Two of the most popular beauty boxes come from none other than Walmart and Target. Other firms are partnering as a channel into the box market. Bergdorf Goodman, for example, partners with beauty player GlossyBox, and Nordstrom recently acquired Trunk Club, which offers individually styled apparel selections for men.

These packages of delight and surprise are only the latest iteration in the ongoing business quest for low-cost, recurring revenue from happy and loyal customers. Subscriptions have been around for a long time, and so have contracts, both of which connect customers and companies over the long term. Software-as-a-service has already swept the software industry, with Microsoft and Adobe moving to the subscription model for key products. But the truth is, our ongoing relationships with the newspapers we subscribe to, the cell phone providers we contract with, and the software makers we rely on don't bring much joy or intimacy. In fact, it mostly feels as if they just want to make sure we pay on time.

Getting your customers to subscribe to you and your product just to get them to open their wallets each month will bring limited success.

Most people don't love paying bills, and locking people into a contract where they have no choice but to subscribe will not increase affinity. But getting your customers to subscribe in order for you to form and develop a positive, two-way relationship provides many advantages on top of more revenue. Customer contributors (principle 5) and the subscription business model are complementary ways of inviting your customers into a mutually beneficial, long-term relationship with your organization.

Take Every Opportunity to Delight

Your customers' lives are busy. The time they spend interacting with your organization is only a minute fraction of their week—although for most firms, it's the only fraction they care about. Building the kind of long-term relationship that supports contribution, and ultimately network orchestration, requires more affinity—on both sides of the relationship—than mere transactions or promotions can provide. On the other hand, a subscription revenue model brings a lot more benefit than simply ongoing and recurring revenue.

Of course, there are financial and operational advantages to subscriptions. Ideally, customer subscriptions provide stable and predictable revenue, something that greatly eases planning, production, and delivery. Further, revenue that comes from a customer you've already acquired is far less expensive than revenue from a new customer, who must be acquired through advertising and marketing. And revenue that was prebooked months ago is better still.

The advantages, however, go deeper than the numbers. Every time your customers interact with your organization, you have an opportunity to increase awareness and hopefully affinity. Amir Elaguizy, founder of Cratejoy, a platform for subscription businesses, says, "Every single month you have another opportunity to say, 'Hey, delighted customer, why don't you tell your friends about how awesome this subscription is?'"[1]

The happy customers of subscription boxes, for example, generate an enormous amount of social media content. "Unboxing" videos, in

which subscribers open, react to, and discuss their monthly packages, are a YouTube phenomenon, and a great deal of content also goes up on blogs, Instagram, and Twitter. Most subscription programs also lend themselves perfectly to referrals, where you get your next installment at a discount if you get a friend to sign up.

The mentality of a subscriber is simply different from that of a transactor. *Transactors* are nonrepeat, efficiency buyers. *Subscribers* know that their relationship with the products and the firm is ongoing, and they have good reason to stay in touch, learn what's happening, and provide feedback. By helping the company understand their individual wants, subscribers can improve the next installment of a product or service they receive—whether it's a feature update to software or a new box of carefully curated chocolates. It's this mental model that helps persuade customers to contribute to the organizations they love.

This brings us to one last benefit of the subscription model: acquiring data. Through regular interactions and touch points with their customer base, subscription companies have a marvelous opportunity to learn more about what their customers want and how they want to engage. Each interaction is an opportunity to experiment with messaging, offer new products, and learn from the results. In contrast, many companies we repeatedly interact with fail to use these opportunities to learn about us as customers. Your family may shop at Whole Foods every week, but the store managers know a lot more about the bananas in their stores than about you. Some patients return to Massachusetts General Hospital every week for treatment, but the hospital still knows its billing codes better than its most frequent patients.

Don't Get Hung Up on Revenue

Although subscription revenue is wonderful, there is also a benefit in having customers subscribe to nonrevenue activities—such as voting for Threadless t-shirt designs each week or reading the funny Trader Joe's flyer—that complement revenue-generating activities. It's easy to

understand the financial benefits of subscription, but the point isn't simply to make your customers keep paying.

For example, despite the recurring revenue we give them, few people feel positively about their cable or cell phone providers. In fact, most of us feel hamstrung by poor customer service and limited choices. In these cases, the lock-in contract only emphasizes to customers that their satisfaction is unimportant and likely will not be served. In contrast, positive externalities, such as increased awareness, engagement, referrals, and participation, result only from positive interactions. The goal is to regularly delight and engage your customer, not just to bill them.

Meeting this goal is certainly possible through activities that don't generate revenue. Getting customers or potential customers to follow your brand on Facebook, LinkedIn, Twitter, Instagram, and so on is a great way to keep customers engaged. Having a useful or entertaining app that sits on people's phones and tablets is another great way to remind them of your organization.

You can find ways to keep people involved by inviting them into the most interesting parts of the company. For example, if we return to the Threadless case study from principle 5, thousands of people visit the site every week just to see the new t-shirt designs and vote on the best ones. We all have opinions, and we love to be asked for them—and if we buy a new shirt in the process, so much the better for Threadless. Co-creation is one of the best ways to keep customers reengaging over time.

Principle 6, Revenues: From Transaction to Subscription

Transaction — Subscription

The sixth principle is to change your customers' relationships with your organization from transaction to subscription. On the left side of the spectrum are companies that transact with their customers at the point of sale and seldom hear from them again until they return on their own

to make another purchase. These firms may advertise and attempt to draw their customers in for repeat sales, but they do not have standard, ongoing two-way dialogue.

On the right side of the spectrum are the companies whose business models rely on subscriptions—ongoing, revenue-generating (and also insight- and affinity-generating) interactions with their customers. In the middle of the spectrum are companies that keep their customers "mentally" subscribed through social media, loyalty programs, opportunities to contribute, and other outreach efforts.

If you want to move to the right and create subscription opportunities for your customers, you need to answer both *what* and *how*. Surprisingly, the question of *what* tends to be the easier part, although it's fairly industry-specific. Your subscription offering could be any of the four asset types.

- Things-based subscriptions include physical goods such as consumer or household products. Subscription boxes like Birchbox and BarkBox fall into this category.
- Service-oriented subscriptions include repair and maintenance, premium customer support, and education. Your lawn service fits this model, as do retainer agreements for legal counsel.
- Information subscriptions include software, product insights, research, and data. Microsoft and Adobe have both moved to subscription services for their software. *Consumer Reports* is another good example.
- Network subscriptions provide access to a platform or group of people. Examples include Angie's List and LinkedIn premium memberships.

What is trickier is the *how*—figuring out how to create a subscription program that results in happy customers, creating both financial and affinity benefits. We've noticed a few themes in organizations that do this well.

SURPRISE AND DELIGHT. The first is that the best subscription models use each interaction to bring joy to their customers, increasing affinity and loyalty steadily over time. You offer, for example, a great customer experience, a beautiful interface, or an unexpected treat or benefit, whether tangible (products) or intangible (information).

One of the many subscription boxes, Phone Case of the Month, delivers stylish new phone cases to its customers on a regular basis. Imagine, instead, if AT&T, Sprint, or Verizon offered this service. For a small fee, their customers could enroll in a "Style My Phone" program in which each month their bill would arrive in the mail paired with a fun new phone case or even some decals. The service providers could partner with Etsy or Threadless to keep the designs fresh and on-trend. How much happier do you think their customers would be when paying their bill each month? And we don't need to stick with the physical world. Other options to delight include free downloads of popular apps, phone-cleaning services, automatic data backup, or funny text messages from popular comedians.

GET DATA. Because increasing intimacy and affiliation is a key goal of subscription models, it's important to use the regular touch point as an opportunity to listen to your customers and adapt your offering. The direct method is simply to ask for feedback during the interaction. Most people love to be asked for their opinions, and many will gladly give feedback if the process is integrated and simple. For example, customer-provided ratings are a key part of the Uber and Airbnb business models.

There's also a great opportunity for indirectly provided data. Each interaction gives the company a chance to gauge customer reaction to various products and services. When Birchbox sends samples to its 800,000 subscribers, it can watch carefully to see how many of them then visit the product pages on the Birchbox e-commerce website and how many make purchases. Birchbox can then figure out whether lipstick is more popular than nail polish, whether mint green is "in" this season, and which age group of women is most likely to use styling mousse in their hair.

By increasing the cadence, and often the variety, of transactions, subscription models provide invaluable data about customers.

PERSONALIZE. What do you do with the data you accumulate? You use it to treat your customers as unique individuals, or groups of one, as Nike does in inviting its customers to design their own sneakers. Deepening the relationship between customers and companies isn't limited to the customer side. Organizations must do their part, too, by learning about their customers and then using what they've learned to improve their communication and offerings.

In general, these approaches suggest that your organization treat customers as complete, interesting, valuable individuals. You build relationships with customers with the same care, attention, and dialogue as you do friends and family in your personal life. We didn't always have the technology to do this. Now we do, and delightful interaction, deep understanding, and tailored offerings are quickly becoming the customer expectation. Now rank your organization on transaction (1) to subscription (10).

Do Subscription Right

Recurring revenues alone do not mean that you've succeeded at subscription. The goal is to get your customers to subscribe not only to paying you, but also to interacting with you and deepening their connection to your firm.

Let's look at the subscription component of a classic business case: Netflix versus Blockbuster. At this point we all know the ending. After nearly thirty years in the video rental business, Blockbuster filed for bankruptcy in January 2014. Netflix is currently eighteen years old, with more than seventy-four million subscribers globally in more than forty countries. There were many reasons that the story ended as it did, but one thing that the two companies had in common is the use of a subscription revenue model.

Netflix and Blockbuster both offered subscription video rental services, but Netflix did a much better job of using the subscription model to build relationships. From the start, Netflix delighted customers with the novelty of DVDs coming to them in their mailboxes. Netflix also requested that their customers review the movies they saw and used this data to return value by suggesting movies aligned with their customer profiles, a classic use of big data to save customers time by doing the research for them. Going into 2014, Netflix had a Net Promoter Score of +54, and Blockbuster on Demand of +11 (a perfect score is +100).

Start Today, Small Is OK

Vitally engaged customers are essential to the valuable network orchestration business model. A subscription model of interaction will help customers return repeatedly. Orchestrated well, with ongoing development of customer relationships—and not customer transactions—as the key performance indicator, each customer revisit will generate greater affinity and value for the customer as well as greater clarity and value to the firm.

PRINCIPLE 7

EMPLOYEES

From Employees to Partners

Employment in society has overstretched itself.

—Charles Handy, author and philosopher

WHEN UBER PASSED THE MILLION-DRIVER MARK (THAT'S right—one million drivers) in late 2015, CEO Travis Kalanick wrote in the *Economist*, "I realised that sharing-economy companies really are pointing the way to a more promising future, where we have more power over when, where and how long to work. It's a shift that has the potential to give people more flexibility, more freedom and more control over their lives, their jobs and their incomes."[1]

One might think that this quotation is self-serving, given that Uber's digital network business model is based on a network of freelance drivers. However, trends indicate that the workforce in general is seeking greater control and flexibility in both life and employment. A recent study by Ernst & Young found that flexibility is a top priority for workers.[2] Given these priorities, it may be that Uber is providing exactly the structure that many are seeking.

A New Model of Employment Is Rising

Think about some of your best and brightest employees—the ones you hope will still be working for you in twenty years. Wouldn't it be wonderful if you could make every employee perform like these high-potential individuals? The answer might be to let them go—and then bring them back as independent workers instead of as employees.

Obviously that's a bit tongue-in-cheek, but a recent study by IBM on independent workers, including contractors, freelancers, and consultants, found that these nonemployees were significantly more engaged than average workers, and nearly at the level of companies' highest performers. On the dimensions of job satisfaction and pride, independent workers actually gave consistently higher ratings than high performers.[3]

In short, the relationship between organizations and their workers is changing. Increasingly, leaders see the benefit of what has been called the *Hollywood model* of employment. Taken from the way teams of specialized individuals come together to work on movie productions, the Hollywood model of employment is short-term, project-based work, where each individual is brought on with targeted expertise to fulfill a specific role.

Adam Davidson, who recently visited a movie set to act as a technical adviser, marveled at the way 150 people who had never worked together formed a unit to work on this film like a well-oiled machine.[4] Costumes, props, lighting, sound, cameras, makeup, hair, acting, directing, design—all worked in complete harmony. It happens on movie sets every day all over the world. Davidson wrote in the *New York Times Magazine*, "There was no transition time; everybody worked together seamlessly, instantly."

Here's Why the Contractor Model Works

Anyone who has worked in the corporate world knows how difficult it is to take a project from inception to implementation. Even the simplest undertakings somehow become epic battles against corporate dragons,

such as competing interests, organizational politics, budget constraints, and plain old inertia. Remarkably, though, a group of independent contractors can sometimes come together efficiently to complete a complex project that an organization might struggle with for years. The Hollywood model, for example, benefits from clear expectations for each role, workers who have specialized expertise, and recurring project opportunities.

It used to be difficult to find available independent workers with the right skills for a particular need, but online networks such as LinkedIn, Upwork, and Guru have dramatically reduced the friction in the contract labor market. Contract workers bring many advantages to an organization. They are flexible resources that can be employed when needed and cost nothing when not being utilized, and they let you try out their skill sets without committing. On top of that, they can actually be more effective than employees in many situations. Here are some of the common reasons.

THEY PROMPT ORGANIZATIONAL CLARITY AND COMMITMENT. You usually exercise more organization oversight when you hire an external worker than when you allocate an employee to a project. An employee is a cost the organization is already expecting to pay, but an independent worker requires an additional financial commitment that usually must be approved. This additional process and scrutiny usually mean that contractors are brought on board only after a specific scope of work has been clarified and deemed important. Once the contractor begins work, the organization will make sure he has everything he needs to be successful so that the extra expense isn't wasted.

WORKERS ARE FOCUSED. With a clear scope of work, an independent worker can bring laser focus to her allocated tasks. Although full-time employees frequently have competing (sometimes contradictory) projects, multiple reporting relationships, and changing corporate agendas to deal with, independent workers can stay focused on fulfilling their scope of work.

THEY BRING UNIQUE EXPERTISE. In most circumstances, independent workers are brought in because their specific capabilities are uniquely suited to a task. In contrast, when projects are staffed with employees, the project manager usually must select from those with bandwidth, rather than those with the perfect skill sets—and we all know how competitive it is to gain the time of the best performers.

THEY HAVE A SENSE OF OWNERSHIP. Compared with employees, contract workers feel more ownership over their work product, often resulting in greater commitment and engagement, per the IBM study cited earlier. For contract workers, both their brand and their future employment are directly tied to their personal output, and they know that every client is a possible reference for the next one. Because of the interconnected nature of companies and teams, it's usually harder to tie the work of employees to individual performance, and full-time employees do not expect to need to prove their capability regularly. In short, the contractor's work builds her own brand; the employee's work builds the company's brand.

A CAUTIONARY TALE. We can pull this all together with a story about two people we'll call contractor Maria and employee John. This may seem like a caricature, but please consider whether you've seen something similar happen in your own organization. The answer likely is yes.

The Acme Company needs to redesign its website. The web team decides to put employee John on the project. Web design is not John's specialty, but his last project recently ended and he has some bandwidth. When the work begins, John struggles to update his knowledge of web design and manage his other ongoing responsibilities. One month in, the inventory management system goes down and John refocuses his effort on fixing it, delaying the web design project by three weeks. Two months in, the project leader quits, and a new leader comes on board with a different vision, requiring a month of rework. John has trouble getting the access he needs from the IT department to properly test the new site, and he's told to wait his turn as IT has a huge backlog. After six

long months the project wraps up. John is not proud of the website, but he is glad it is finished.

Now let's roll back the clock and consider a different scenario. This time the Acme Company decides to use contractor Maria. Web design is Maria's specialty and passion. She and the web team collaborate to create a specific scope of work that Maria then focuses on completing, with little competing for her attention. When the new project leader comes on board, Maria quotes him the increased cost of her time for rework; he decides not to change the scope of the project. When Maria needs access from the IT department, her request is expedited because slowing her down costs the company money. The project is completed in three months. Maria is proud to add it to her portfolio and share it with her next potential client. The new project leader is happy to be a reference for her stellar work.

We have seen these scenarios play out over and over again. Although the answer is not as simple as "switch your employment model to 100 percent independent workers," independent relationships offer many attributes that benefit both the organization and the worker.

What Do Workers Want?

We've documented how independent workers (partners, rather than employees) can be good for employers, but this working arrangement also proves to be good for the workers themselves. New generations of workers, as expected, have different wants and needs from those of earlier workers. Millennials entering the workforce, and many of us a bit older, have become accustomed to autonomy, choice, and influence. The same networks that reduce friction for recruiting companies also reduce friction for workers looking for their next great role. Individuals can interact with and influence their favorite brands through Facebook and Twitter, so why wouldn't they expect to be influencers at work as well? They do—but only a few enlightened employers are providing what employees need to feel empowered, developed, and influential in their jobs.

A recent Gallup poll found that more than 70 percent of US employees are not engaged in their jobs—meaning that they are not "involved in, enthusiastic about, and committed to their work and workplace."[5] Ouch. And it's not only employees. Research by Rosalind Bergemann found that 74 percent of workers who voluntarily chose to become independent cited a lack of *employer* engagement as their principal reason for leaving.[6] Reinforcing this point, Mike Myatt, author of *Hacking Leadership*, found that more than 70 percent of employees don't feel valued or appreciated by their employers.[7]

Add to this dysfunctional relationship a few more facts. What millennials want most for their careers is meaningful work, and the two benefits millennials most value are (1) training and development and (2) flexible working hours. Common benefits of employment, such as health care, vacation, and child care, trail far behind in desirability.[8] No wonder 34 percent of the American workforce has already shifted to independent work; they want to serve themselves, develop themselves, control themselves, and ultimately find the work that makes them happy.

The burgeoning independent workforce changes things for organizations and for employees. Some of these changes are tactical, such as finding new ways for workers to get health care, and others are relational, such as figuring out how to help your workers find fulfillment. But there is a great win-win possible. In the best of all worlds, workers find fulfilling work that provides the control, development, and meaning they desire, and employers benefit from an efficient and engaged workforce.

Principle 7, Employees: From Employees to Partners

Employees ——— Partners

The seventh principle of creating network value is to shift at least a portion of your workers from employees to partners. On the left side of the scale are traditional organizations that rely primarily on long-term,

full-time employees who are managed in the customary way, with relatively little autonomy. On the right side of the spectrum are companies that rely heavily on partnering with an independent workforce or that create a culture of empowered autonomy within a traditional workforce.

Many of the partnering firms employ new business models that leverage a network to source their primary workforce. Airbnb, Uber, Etsy, and eBay are examples of companies in which nonemployees are the essential value creators. Although we don't usually think of it this way, most of us Facebook and LinkedIn users are also nonemployees, trading our content for access to the platforms.

In the middle sit companies who still mostly have employees but are working to treat them as independent partners. And we don't mean by cutting employee benefits. We mean by giving their employees a greater degree of autonomy, flexibility, development, and overall a greater degree of control and influence. Here is where the co-creator leader lets go a little more.

There are many ways to begin shifting your organization to the right end of the spectrum. Google's 20 percent time policy (or 3M's 15 percent time, if you'd like to go back further)—where workers are encouraged to invest the allotted percentage of their time in their own projects and ideas that they think will be most valuable to the company—are wonderful examples. AT&T has an internal idea stock market called the Innovation Pipeline (TIP), where employees can pitch and vote on ideas, choosing the best to be presented to senior leaders. Deloitte has developed a new approach to human resources that it calls *mass career customization*, with the goal of giving employees more control over their career progress, letting them ramp up or ramp down and make moves as needed to fit their current life situation.

Companies that treat their employees as independent, skilled, valuable partners are actually practicing network orchestration with an internal network—their workforce. Promoting greater ownership and independence by your employees allows them to operate as partners who contribute rather than subordinates who do what they're told. If

employees feel that their work contributes to their personal brand and esteem, on top of their bank accounts, they will act differently.

There are many ways to create a relationship with your workforce that enables rather than controls. Most companies fall in the middle of the spectrum. To help pinpoint where your organization sits between employee (1) and partner (10), consider these questions:

- How much worker development do you offer (training, tuition reimbursement, etc.), and how much control does the worker have over the training he receives?
- How flexible are your career paths? Can a worker easily move from one division or role to another? Who controls his career path—the worker or the organization?
- Do workers have flexibility in the hours or locations of their work? Does your organization have a culture of face time? (If workers are regularly in the office after working hours, the answer is yes.)
- If a worker has a great idea for the firm, even in an area where he doesn't work, how much support is he given? How likely is it that the idea will reach the attention of upper management?
- Do your workers have a mission that they can find meaning in? (Not every company can feed the world's children, but every company can create a mission that people can understand, relate to, and espouse.)

If you want to know how to create a workforce with a more independent culture, simply revisit each of the foregoing questions and think about what would work in your organization to deliver more development, flexibility, influence, and inspiration to your employees.

Here's another idea as well: ask your employees to tell you what would make their work experience better for them. Their answers might surprise you.

One Person Performs Many Roles

One of the themes of the network world is that roles of all kinds are merging. Customers, employees, partners, and owners used to be distinct groups. But now we're beginning to recognize that each individual—each of us—can play all of these roles, and sometimes for the same company.

We've discussed the blurred lines between customers and employees that arise through co-creation, and between employees and partners through the independent workforce. But employees can also be owners. Of course, contract workers own their own work and personal brand, but your employees can also be made to feel and behave like owners, and the benefits can be significant. How many times have we all heard executives lament a lack of employee buy-in? A sense of ownership solves that problem.

Frank Budwey owns a grocery store in North Tonawanda, New York. Or should we say co-owns? After the untimely death of his son, Budwey decided to give the store's thirty-three full-time employees just shy of 50 percent ownership in the supermarket, allowing each employee to begin pocketing a share of the store's profit. As you might expect, employee morale soared, and sales took the same path—rising as much as 20 percent year over year.

Of course they did. Budwey couldn't have done much more to align the interests of his employees with the success of the store. Their brands are now the same, and the benefits are shared. It's a wonderful model.

Now Don't Fire Everybody

It's important to emphasize that an independent partner workforce is not a one-size-fits-all solution. Some workers will always want the stability of a full-time, long-term position, and some roles will always need to be filled by those who hold the long-term well-being of the organization as the priority. You may never convert to a fully contract workforce,

but you may find an unexpected way to align your interests with those of an external network, resulting in a new, independent source of value for your company.

Please don't ignore the fundamental changes that are affecting the relationship between workers and organizations. Workers have new needs—and new capability to move around until they find an employment arrangement that suits them. Companies that meet these new needs will find that they, too, benefit from an inspired, happy, contributing workforce. Those that fail to meet worker needs will see their best and brightest head off in search of their next great role.

PRINCIPLE 8

MEASUREMENT

From Accounting to Big Data

Not everything that counts can be counted,
and not everything that can be counted counts.

—William Bruce Cameron, sociologist

YOU MIGHT NOT EXPECT A CHAIN OF BARBECUE JOINTS WITH eleven people on its information technology staff to be an innovator in the use of big data. If so, you're in for a surprise. Big data isn't just for the Googles, Apples, Amazons, and Facebooks.

Using big data doesn't have to be a complicated, resource-heavy, year-long endeavor. Big data, for our purposes, is nothing more than large sets of information that can be analyzed to understand useful patterns, often, but not always, related to human behavior.

Husband-and-wife team Roland Dickey (CEO) and Laura Dickey (CIO) run Dickey's Barbecue Pit, with 514 restaurants across the United States. They wanted to bring big data to barbecue, so they partnered with an external business intelligence firm to provide and develop a custom solution they call Smoke Stack.[1]

Smoke Stack gathers and analyzes data from a range of sources, including point-of-sale systems, loyalty programs, customer surveys, and inventory systems, to provide a nearly real-time dashboard of sales and performance information. The internal team reviews this data every twenty minutes and reviews daily trends each morning. With this timely and complete data, Dickey's can address performance issues of all sorts very quickly. For example, if labor costs spike in one location, the operations team can be sent in to help. If another restaurant is accumulating a backlog of unsold ribs, Dickey's can text a promotion to loyal customers in the area.

Laura Dickey explains that big data is a critical element in any competitive business.

> If a region or store is above or below a KPI—whether it is labor or cost of goods—we can deploy resources to course-correct, and we are reacting to those numbers every 12 to 24 hours instead of at the end of every business week or in some cases using months-old data. To stay profitable, it is just not reasonable to do business that way any more.[2]

Laura Dickey is right. It's not reasonable to run a business with outdated information any more. We can do better.

New Kinds of Assets Need a New Approach to Data

We can assert with confidence that you probably don't have the data you need to best run your businesses. There are three basic ways that most firms fail to make the most of their measurement and tracking systems.

THEY DON'T MEASURE THE RIGHT THINGS. Traditional measurement systems focus almost exclusively on physical things, but, as we've discussed, there are four primary types of assets: things, people, ideas, and networks. Of course, nearly all firms in the United States follow

generally accepted accounting principles. GAAP does a good job with physical assets, but it does not have a good track record with people, ideas, or networks. Employees, which many firms count as their greatest asset, are actually accounted for as expenses (no wonder there is decreasing loyalty between employees and employers). Ideas and other intellectual property can sometimes, but not always, be capitalized. Networks are basically ignored, although sometimes customer sentiment can be captured in the asset known as goodwill.

Admittedly, GAAP isn't the beginning or the end of measurement for most organizations, but it certainly places a focus on physical assets, for which it is easier to assign hard values. For firms that report to their stakeholders regularly using a format that emphasizes the physical, it's hard not to focus on physical assets exclusively. It's also extremely difficult to measure intangible assets. For example, measuring customer sentiment was much harder in the days before social media and big data, and it's still difficult to value definitively.

However, if you're not measuring your people, ideas, and networks, you're thwarting yourself competitively. Research by Ocean Tomo found that intangible assets now make up 84 percent of the S&P 500 market value, up from only 17 percent in 1975 (when GAAP would have been a lot more useful).[3]

THEY PAY TOO LITTLE ATTENTION TO THE EXTERNAL. The second factor is that most traditional measures are internally focused. Companies watch sales numbers, inventory, manufacturing productivity, employee productivity, and all the things they think most affect their success—forgetting that a great, and sometimes greater, source of value exists in external ideas and networks. Gaining a better understanding of your network members—what they want, what they have to offer, and how they want to interact with your organization—is key to becoming a network orchestrator.

Loyalty programs are an easy first step in getting external data, as are social media platforms like Facebook, LinkedIn, and Twitter. The tricky

part is getting and using the data, and luckily there are resources to help you. For example, Topsy, recently acquired by Apple, helps companies draw insights from activity on social media, and iSentium helps companies tap in to investor network sentiment and determine whether the results are positive or negative for their stock.[4]

Companies and their external networks are becoming tightly intertwined, with the result that external networks of alumni, customers, investors, and communities have more power than ever to influence organizations. Understanding the status of these networks—as well as their affinities, activities, and trajectories—is essential to understanding the position of your firm.

THEY'RE NOT TIMELY. Third, the data that organizations report often arrives a month or more after it was gathered. This time gap is unacceptable, because it may prevent you from taking corrective action or seizing an opportunity. Let's assume, for example, that a downturn in a local economy leads to belt-tightening and retailers start seeing reduced foot traffic. A retailer with a real-time, integrated, big data dashboard might notice the decline in sales after a week and start adjusting staffing and product shipping. Another retailer doesn't react to this trend until a month's (or even two months') worth of data rolls into headquarters. At that point the inventory storerooms are overflowing and the staffing costs have been out of line for more than a month. Slow reactions like this one can cost a company hundreds of thousands of dollars.

And it's a matter not only of minimizing downside but also of maximizing upside. Companies with access to nearly real-time data, and particularly external data, will notice opportunities that others will miss. For example, Caesars casino has long had a customer loyalty program, but recently it began to integrate customer data with in-casino activity to identify patterns.[5] One opportunity it identified: if a new loyalty program member has a run of bad luck at the slots, he will likely not return to the casino. The odds of an ongoing relationship are greatly improved, however, if Caesars presents that customer with a free meal

coupon or some other token while he is still in the casino. A real-time, integrated, big data system allows Caesars to take advantage of these opportunities.

These three factors—measuring all assets, looking outward, and using real-time data—create great competitive advantage. As Laura Dickey said, it's just not reasonable to do business without big data.

Principle 8, Measurement: From Accounting to Big Data

Accounting ▬▬▬ Big data

The eighth principle is to shift from basic accounting data, focused on the physical and having significant time delays, to big data analytics—including intangible, external assets and real-time analysis. On the left side of the measurement spectrum are organizations that count up their property, plant, and equipment, tally them in spreadsheets, e-mail them to finance, and report once a month. On the right side of the spectrum are companies that still measure all the physical stuff, usually in close to real time, but also track their external, intangible assets and use this data to improve the speed and quality of decision making.

Big data is one of the hardest principles to implement because implementing it requires infrastructure as well as specific technical skill sets. Consider the following habits of companies that use big data well, and rank yourself from accounting (1) to big data (10).

START WITH CLEAR GOALS. The essential first step is to understand exactly what data would be useful to you and how you intend to use it. Too many big data business plans follow this format:

Step 1: Gather lots of data.

Step 2: Analyze the data.

Step 3: Profit.

No part of this plan is specific enough to create value for the company. Gathering and combining data (for example, sales data with loyalty program profiles) is expensive and time-consuming, as is analyzing the data. So you want to know exactly what your goal is for this endeavor. For example, you may want to better understand how customers use your product in order to determine which new functions will be most valued. Or you may want to track product sales in real time in order to better allocate inventory and avoid stock-outs.

A good place to look for big data opportunities is in your firm's most significant intangible assets. These are often undermanaged.

GET THE RIGHT TALENT. Exploiting big data requires unique skills. Merely integrating the appropriate IT systems is difficult, although your IT team may be up to the task. Analyzing the data, however, is a significant task, requiring specialized data analysts and statisticians. You may have a great spreadsheet expert, but big data specialists can do language parsing, self-evolving algorithms, cluster analysis, and much more.

There are many full-service options, particularly for simple, common requests such as summarizing the general Twitter sentiment of your stock or company. But for anything more complicated, you need talent of your own who can understand the specifics and intricacies of your operations and iterate with the management team on the insights.

USE THE INSIGHTS. You wouldn't go to all the trouble and expense of creating a big data capability, or partnering with a provider, if you didn't intend to analyze and use the data. Making the best use of big data, however, may require changing some of your management practices. For example, you may need to empower decision making at a lower level to take advantage of the real-time nature of your new dashboards. The leadership team may also have to create general heuristics, rather than specific guidance, to allow people in the organization to make use of the data independently while still following a company-wide approach.

If you try to manage the organization in the same way, taking in and reacting to the wealth of granular information yourself (or within your leadership team), you will most likely become a bottleneck, limiting the potential of big data in your organization. Make sure your organization is able to actually use the insights in a timely way.

It's Not Only for Facebook and Twitter

It's easy to think of big data within the context of social media, and in industries that maintain direct consumer relationships, such as retailing. But big data can yield big insight in any industry, even if it's applied mostly to basic, physical assets.

Farming is a great example, because it's very physical, and not very brand- or customer-oriented. One of the most exciting big data startups of 2015 was Granular, which creates farm-management software that integrates all parts of the business, from hardware such as tractors, drones, and scales, to business operations such as budgeting and employee activity, to weather and environmental data. Backed by big investors like Andreessen Horowitz and Google Ventures, Granular promises to revolutionize farming—increasing productivity and allowing farmers to understand the performance of each crop and each field and even each cloud in real time.

Continuing in the agriculture theme, John Deere is another surprise player in the big data revolution. The company created a self-driving vehicle long before Google did, although navigating a field is admittedly easier than driving on city streets. John Deere also made an early leap into the internet of things by connecting its farm equipment with a network of sensors that can help coordinate movement, map fields, and gather crop data. Combined with external data such as current and historical weather patterns, and even information about other farmers who permit their data to be shared, John Deere provides farmers with detailed recommendations on everything from what and when to plant to how to deploy and service machinery.

If everyone from tractor manufacturers to barbecue joints and casinos to retailers can put big data to good use, you can, too—and you probably should do so sooner rather than later.

Join the Adventure of Big Data and Analytics

Big data isn't a magic word, or even a magic concept. It's simply a tool, and one that allows us to learn things about our companies and our customers (and more) that we would have loved to have known decades ago. We just got used to doing without that information for those same decades.

But now the digital age is here to stay, and we have the ability to know and make use of detailed and interesting information about the world we live in. It's a wonderful opportunity to improve operations, decrease waste, and better serve our customers and the world. It's time to figure out what opportunities are most exciting for you and your organization, and start the big data adventure.

PRINCIPLE 9

BOARDS

From Governance to Representation

We need diversity of thought in the world
to face the new challenges.

—Tim Berners-Lee, inventor of the World Wide Web

IT'S NOT EASY TO MANAGE A COMPANY YOU DON'T UNDERSTAND. IN 2000, Kellogg Company, known for popular brands such as Froot Loops, Pop-Tarts, Frosted Flakes, and Pringles, purchased a small food company called Kashi. Kashi was a start-up that played in a similar part of the food market as Kellogg—with cereals, snack bars, crackers, and prepared foods—but Kashi had a mission focused on nutritious, plant-based foods and sustainable, ethical farming practices. One of Kashi's taglines is "7 Whole Grains on a Mission."

The purchase of Kashi seemed like a great move on Kellogg's part, a few years ahead of the dramatic growth in the health and natural foods market in the late 2000s. Carlos Gutierrez, then Kellogg CEO, gave the Kashi team plenty of space to maintain its own culture and principles while still operating within the Kellogg umbrella. Kashi did very well, leveraging broad Kellogg's resources to grow revenues 25-fold by 2008.

However, around this time Kellogg began to pull Kashi more closely into the fold and align it with the rest of the corporation. Product planning, procurement, and manufacturing all began to follow the broader Kellogg processes, and that slowed Kashi's innovation pipeline. Kellogg combined the two sales teams, and Kashi began to target "regular" consumers as well as the health-conscious market. Then things started to stall. Many of Kashi's long-term employees left, feeling that the firm had lost its mission and entrepreneurial spirit, and customers began to defect to brands that stayed current with the latest health trends.

It's easy to assume that the governors of an organization—the executives and board members with many years of experience—know best. In truth, however, often they are disconnected from their key networks—including employees and customers—in values as well as life experiences. Organizations succeed when the leaders understand and represent the interests and priorities of their key networks.

In this case, misalignment in governance meant that Kashi was slow to catch on to the non-GMO (genetically modified organism) and gluten-free trends, and the brand's credibility was seriously hurt when news came out that Kellogg had contributed hundreds of thousands of dollars to a campaign that opposed the labeling of GMO foods—a cause supported by many customers in the natural food market. In 2014 alone, revenues from Kashi's biggest category, ready-to-eat cereal, dropped 21 percent.

Now Kellogg is working to turn Kashi around and govern it in a way that will again enable it to innovate quickly and hold to the mission and values of its target market. Kellogg has great resources to help the smaller brand, but as current Kellogg CEO John Bryant said, "A large organization can sometimes help too much."[1]

You Need to Correct the Great Mismatch

There is a great mismatch between those who manage, govern, and advise businesses and the employees, customers, and networks of those organizations, and this mismatch hurts companies. In the case

of Kashi, the processes that the leadership team supported for the rest of the organization hampered Kashi's ability to innovate and stay in touch with its core market. Further, the values of the Kellogg board and executives were out of sync with the values of Kashi's team and, more importantly, its customers. These types of conflicts, these misalignments, between the governors and the rest of us who work, buy, and invest, are only growing.

Every year Spencer Stuart develops the US Board Index report, which reviews the latest trends in board composition and practices in the S&P 500 companies. Here are some highlights from 2014:

- Some 19 percent of directors are women.
- Fourteen percent of directors are minorities (in the largest two hundred companies).
- Eight percent of directors are of non-US origin (in the largest two hundred companies).
- The average tenure of a director is 8.7 years.
- The median age of a director is sixty-three.[2]

In addition, our own research found that only 12 percent of directors have technical or digital expertise.

Now let's take a look at the US population—the shoppers, workers, and communities that support these companies.

- Women make up 51 percent of the population and control more than 70 percent of consumer spending.[3]
- Minorities constitute 27 percent of the population.
- Thirteen percent of the population is foreign born, and in 2013, 33 percent of revenue for the S&P 500 was from foreign sales.[4]
- The median age in the United States is thirty-six, and only 13 percent of the population is age sixty-five or older.

- The PricewaterhouseCoopers 2014 US CEO survey found that 86 percent of CEOs believe technology will transform their businesses in the next five years.[5]

Can you spot the mismatch? Perhaps we should say "complete misalignment." On every statistic, boards are not representative of the key stakeholder groups of the companies they advise. Demographically, boards are quite different from their current customers and their hoped-for future customers. Few boards have the digital technology savvy to support a technology transformation in their companies. Boards cannot hope to make informed decisions when their members are so far from the demographics they serve, and equally far from the technology needed to reach these demographic groups—particularly if the members aren't able to adapt their own mental models.

We would never assert that there should be perfect alignment between the governors and the market. Directors, executives, and advisers do need a great deal of business experience and acumen—much more than the average customer or employee might attain. On the other hand, the most successful companies are the ones that look outward, understand their networks, and create mutually beneficial relationships with them. This is different from the often singularly internal, operational focus of the past few decades, and it requires board members who better represent and understand the firm's networks.

Credit Suisse studied the impact of gender diversity on boards in 2014 and found that when boards had gender diversity, their firms enjoyed higher returns on equity, higher price/book valuations, and higher payout ratios than those led by less diverse boards.[6] McKinsey studied board diversity in 2010 and saw similar results. Boards in the top quartile of diversity, in terms of gender and nationality, saw return on equity 53 percent higher, and earnings before interest and tax 14 percent higher, than boards in the bottom quartile.[7]

This should not surprise us. One of the key capabilities of network orchestration, and for simply thriving in any business model, is building deep

intimacy with networks in order to gain their contributions, serve them as they want to be served (that usually involves a lot of digital technology), and create mutually beneficial relationships. This is difficult to do when the life experience of your board, executives, and advisers is vastly different from that of your key networks. And—not to be politically incorrect, but to name things as they are—the companies that solely employ, serve, and interact with retired white American males are few and far between.

It's also important to address the technology gap directly. Even though business model disruption and digital technology capabilities are top concerns, 80 percent of boards have no digital representation, according to executive search firm Russell Reynolds.[8] Research by the Conference Board and Stanford found that only about 10 percent of boards use social media to engage with stakeholders, and fewer than 8 percent of boards receive reports on their firms' social media use.[9] Given these numbers, it's no surprise that only about a quarter of boards are supportive of, and involved in, digital business initiatives.[10]

Principle 9: From Governance to Representation

Governance ▭ Representation

The ninth principle is to move your firm's leadership team from governance to representation. Another way to look at it might be from oligarchy to democracy. On the left side of the network orchestrator spectrum are organizations whose executives, boards of directors, and other advisers are relatively homogenous. They usually have thirty or more years' worth of work experience focused on the operations that happen within a company, but little experience reaching outward. None of them are digital or technology specialists, and most do not even use Facebook, LinkedIn, or Twitter.[11] These types of advisers are governors; they create strategy and policy from the top down, relying on their own experience. They do not have many shared experiences with the company's workers, customers, or the broader community—their firms' networks.

On the right side of the spectrum are organizations whose executives, boards, and other advisers bring a great diversity of perspective and represent the networks in and around the organization. The leadership team probably includes women, minorities, and foreign nationals. It will certainly include digital experts, ready to help design and support new digital strategies, and the makeup of the board may change more rapidly than that of others, with new directors being appointed closer to the rate of market change.

From left to right, the job of the board of directors is to guide the company's policies and objectives, but we have found, as have many research organizations, that those on the right side do a better job of it. Heterogeneous and representative leaders are better able to understand, connect with, and tap in to the networks, and thereby the value, that exist around their organizations. Consider where you fall on the governance (1) to representation (10) spectrum.

Clearly, the goal is to have a diverse, representative, and digital-savvy board of directors and leadership team. If you don't have a board of directors, just replace that term with "advisers." Finding the right people, however, is a long-term goal. You need to start on that now, and there are other things you can do in the meantime.

GET THE MOST OUT OF WHAT YOU HAVE. If your board currently sits on the left side of the spectrum, you can't change its demographics or work experience at once, but you can begin to shift the members' mental models. Some boards are going to "digital boot camp" to learn about the do's and don'ts, risks and rewards of digital technology. Others use reverse mentoring (as once mandated by Jack Welch) to get in touch with the priorities and preferences of those they represent.

BRING DIVERSITY AT A LOWER LEVEL. If you're having trouble finding the right digital director for your board, set your gaze lower, at least for the short term: recruit a chief digital officer for the executive team. The technology know-how will benefit you at any level.

CHANGE THE BAR. One reason boards struggle with diversity is that a common requirement for membership is previous board experience. You can see how this would lock out underrepresented groups almost immediately. Years of work experience is another tricky requirement; someone who came of age in the digital era doesn't have thirty years of leadership experience. This is not even remotely lowering the bar; instead, it is changing the bar to prioritize diversity of thought, experience, and capability.

SET SPECIFIC GOALS. Goals are motivating, and they also tell everyone else where you're going. Adidas set hard targets to increase the number of women managers on the leadership team. By 2012, it had hit 30 percent. The goal for 2015 is 35 percent. This certainly would not have happened if the executive team had thought, "I hope we find more women to be managers next year."[12]

Most boards appoint only one or two new members every year, so be sure that your appointments really count. Changing the culture and representation of your board is certainly possible.

How Macy's Does It

You might expect Macy's, as a 156-year-old retailer, to have a traditional, homogenous governing board. It doesn't. Macy's has one of the most diverse boards in the world.

On Macy's board sit twelve directors. Half are women. (In contrast, fewer than 1 percent of *Fortune* 500 companies have gender parity on their boards.) Recent appointments include forty-six-year-old Annie Young-Scrivner, a Starbucks executive and president of Teavana, who had no previous board experience; and Sara Levinson, an entrepreneur who founded KANDU, which brings together kids and technology to create fun things. Additionally, two members of the Macy's board are African American, one is Hispanic, and one is Asian American.

This has not happened through serendipity. CEO Terry Lundgren has made a concerted effort to recruit highly talented individuals who also bring a diverse perspective to the board. Macy's board member Craig Weatherup puts it this way:

> Boards that aren't looking for younger, digitally savvy female and ethnic board members are really going to fall behind. It's a key part of staying relevant in today's market. I agree that if you're just looking for a sitting CEO or a recently retired CEO it is almost impossible. But there is no reason why that stat should be a limiting criteria.[13]

And how is Macy's doing under the leadership of this diverse board? It is thriving. In 2014, Macy's delivered stock returns that handily beat those of Walmart, Best Buy, and Amazon.com. Macy's has moved much faster than many of its competitors to leverage digital technologies. It developed a strong omnichannel platform that includes real-time inventory; in-store pickup for online purchases; a mobile app that integrates payment, loyalty programs, and local store inventories; and lightning-fast delivery options. Macy's has recently partnered with Li & Fung to explore retailing in China. L2, a research firm that delivers business intelligence related to digital technology, rates Macy's as a "genius" in its Digital IQ Index.[14]

Start with What You're Missing

As you begin the journey toward a leadership team that represents the interests, passions, and expectations of your networks, we encourage you to think about the networks themselves. This includes not only the ones your company currently relates to—your customers, employees, and investors—but also those that you want to build relationships with down the road. Some of the world's most exciting companies—Google, Facebook, Apple—serve almost everyone in the world. That's a lot of people to represent.

So think about the people in those networks, both who they are and what they value, and reflect on how well your current leaders understand and represent them. The biggest gaps are the best places to start. Now you have a new bar that board candidates, executives, and advisers need to meet. It may not be CEO experience, but instead something even more valuable to an organization looking to grow in the digital, networked world.

PRINCIPLE 10

MINDSET

From Closed to Open

Entrepreneurial business favors the open mind.
It favours people whose optimism drives them to prepare for many possible futures, pretty much purely for the joy of doing so.

—Richard Branson, The Virgin Group

EVEN A HUNDRED-YEAR-OLD ORGANIZATION CAN INNOVATE ITS business model. General Motors (GM) is coming enthusiastically, albeit a bit late, to the innovative ride-sharing market with a $500 million investment in Lyft as part of Lyft's latest $1 billion venture financing round. Although a shift from car ownership to car sharing, and even further to autonomous vehicles, could be a risky disruption to their market, GM's leaders have decided to embrace the changing business model landscape in transportation and innovate what they do and how they do it. Daniel Ammann, GM's president, said, "We think there's going to be more change in the world of mobility in the next five years than there has been in the last 50," and GM is getting ready for that change.[1]

From that perspective, Lyft is an excellent partner who will help GM turn their views of the market upside down. Lyft's president John Zimmer stated, "We strongly believe that autonomous vehicle go-to-market strategy is through a network, not through individual car ownership." According to executives at both GM and Lyft, they will start work on developing a network of self-driving vehicles—a challenge to Google, Tesla, and Uber, which are also devoting resources to this innovation.[2]

Openness Makes Space for Ongoing Change

Will GM's self-driving-car aspiration create value for the firm? Will its investment in Lyft lead to automotive leadership in ten years? We couldn't say. But so far its openness to adaptation and new ideas shows potential for future growth and transformation.

We've now reached the last of the principles to be considered for a network orchestrator business model, and it points us to the mental model. Whereas the first nine principles emphasize specific shifts that network orchestrators make in order to better enable their outward-looking, co-creative business models, the final principle is about your own openness to making these shifts and to taking in and adapting to new information in general—whether it's from your customers, employee groups, or the market.

Further, not only do you, and your leadership team, need to be receptive to new ways of thinking, but also you must structure your organization and your life so that you actually receive new ways of thinking. Leaders usually have no shortage of people who are able and willing to agree with their ideas and reinforce their perceptions. It takes effort to find ways to bring new ideas to your awareness, and even more effort to make them a part of what you do.

We should be clear that not everything must change dramatically, and not all at once. When it comes to the principles of network orchestration, every firm will have, and should have, a unique profile—one

that reflects the interaction between a new world and a new market, and the firm's unique history, focus, organizational model, and competitive context. We don't recommend that you abandon your current assets, leadership style, customer relationships, employees, and revenue models, and build a new organization based entirely on network principles. A slash-and-burn approach will only create chaos. What we recommend instead is conscious, incremental, deliberate, ongoing openness and adaptation.

Openness will allow you to develop a portfolio of useful practices that will make your organization more adaptable and valuable in the digital network age. Just as financial portfolios require diversification and balance, your organization should leverage a mix of new ideas and methods, including tangible and intangible assets, employees and freelancers, accounting and big data analytics, and so on. You can develop this degree of openness even within a single core business—by using different approaches to serving the same customer need.

Principle 10, Mindset: From Closed to Open

The tenth principle moves your organization, and the leadership team's mental models, from closed to open. *Closed organizations* define themselves rigidly and have a preference for sticking to their knitting. These types of companies see their customers as product consumers and miss the potential for co-creation. Internally, they keep teams siloed, and they see their employees as worker bees, failing to leverage the innovative capabilities of their workforce. Leaders of closed organizations don't see why digital technology is important when their core business is real estate, or boxes, or mortgages, or soda, and therefore they rarely break out of traditional industry boundaries.

Open organizations, sitting on the other side of the spectrum, think about roles, processes, products, and industries less rigidly. Openness

brings a mental model and a culture of openness and inclusiveness. This perspective provides a lot of flexibility for the organization to adapt to individual needs and broad market changes. Customers who want to develop long-term, co-creative relationships have the option to do so. Leaders may sometimes command, but they also have the capability and the desire to co-create and to help their workforce interact and innovate. Accounting data and big data analytics are used together to drive insight and decision making. Open organizations may not create network capability in every dimension discussed in this book, but they select what is most meaningful within their organizations and with their networks, and they start there.

Being an open organization has become increasingly important as the pace of change has accelerated and business models have evolved. For several reasons, open organizations are more adaptable when technologies and markets begin to shift, and technologies and markets are shifting at a previously unimagined velocity. Here's why open organizations do better.

THEIR INNOVATION PIPELINE IS BROADER. Because they enable communication across silos, open organizations receive new ideas from a much wider variety of sources than do closed organizations. Customers share insights and co-create, employees are empowered at all levels, and other networks, such as suppliers and distributors, are able to contribute as well. A diverse group of innovators is much more likely to bring a novel solution to a tricky problem than is a leadership team with decades of narrow, historical, industry-specific experience.

THEY BEGIN WITH A PORTFOLIO. Open organizations tend to develop a lot of seeds, and their seeds fall further from the core business than those of closed organizations. This portfolio of more diverse initiatives or business units gives open organizations an in-place platform for growth and adaptation when the market shifts. Rather than start from square one each time, open organizations often have something

they have been nurturing, or at least pondering, that can help bridge the gap when disruption hits a key business. Open organizations have a portfolio mindset.

THEIR TALENT POOL IS BALANCED. Open organizations are aware that institutional memory and historicity have value, but they also know that members who come from outside with different experiences bring a vitality that makes a difference. These team members, not to be ageist, most often are younger, and they *arrive* with different mental models than the ones used by those with "experience." Both are valued by the open organization.

THE CULTURE SUPPORTS CHANGE. Because open organizations have a culture that is broad rather than narrow, and open rather than protective, new ideas are more likely to take root and find support to grow.

Where does your company fall on the spectrum from closed to open? Consider the following questions:

- Is our mission statement narrow and focused on a specific industry or product? Or is it broad and focused on serving a large need?
- What percentage of our business comes from our core, and how narrowly is that defined?
- What percentage of our business comes from outside our core, and how far does it depart from the core?
- Is our leadership team excited by and receptive to new ideas, even those outside their areas of expertise?
- How do new ideas reach the leadership team? How easy is it for employees and customers to have their ideas heard?
- Do we understand the digital alternatives to our current business model?

Moving your mindset from closed (1) to open (10), you truly take on the mental model of a network orchestrator. Open organizations create the space needed to encourage network participation and the flexibility to adapt and experiment until they hit a business model that creates mutual value.

Open Can Be Big

Some of the best examples of open organizations are also some of the biggest and most well-known companies in the world. An open perspective is perfect for growth—because everyone is a potential customer or contributor, and every market provides a new opportunity. Open organizations often focus on platforms and customers, rather than industries and products. Open organizations don't need to own everything and keep it within their walls; they can access assets that exist outside the organization.

We have talked about Facebook, but Google is another classic open organization. From its policy of encouraging employees to work 20 percent of their time on their own projects—whatever they think will benefit the company—to its mission to "organize the world's information and make it universally accessible and useful," to its eagerness to take on projects (such as self-driving cars and glucose-checking contact lenses) far outside its core competencies, it could be said that Google has openness in its DNA.

In fact, Google has become so open that founders Larry Page and Sergey Brin have had to create a newer, bigger company—Alphabet—as a part of continuous business model innovation. As Page said in the Alphabet announcement, "We've long believed that over time companies tend to get comfortable doing the same thing, just making incremental changes. But in the technology industry, where revolutionary ideas drive the next big growth areas, you need to be a bit uncomfortable to stay relevant."[3]

We take the point that the technology industry has enveloped other industries at such a rapid rate that it's less like an industry and more like an underlying capability that every business needs. Even so, Page's advice about being a bit uncomfortable to stay relevant applies to open organizations, and especially to open leaders. Closed investors and leaders have seen the risks of complacency and stagnation in the disruptive environment that has become the norm for business.

Amazon.com is another big, open organization. With its mission—"to be earth's most customer-centric company; to build a place where people can come to find and discover anything they might want to buy online"—Amazon has set its sights on nearly every industry one can imagine. Although it started with a simple physical product—books—you can now buy anything you might need from Amazon.com, from web hosting services to streaming videos, to cutting-edge tablets, and a lot more. Amazon also partners with sellers all over the world and allows its customers to sell on the website, too.

Now you may raise the point that some of Amazon's other practices don't seem very open. In *The Everything Store: Jeff Bezos and the Age of Amazon,* CEO Bezos is described as "a micromanager with rigorous standards who is often uninterested in other people's opinions."[4] To this, we reemphasize that each of the principles must be applied carefully, with consideration for *your* firm and the networks *you* are serving. You don't need to shift to the far right edge of the business model spectrum on every principle discussed in this book, but you should consider each one deliberately and conscientiously to determine which will produce the greatest difference, and thereby the most value, for your organization.

We understand that not many companies are like Google and Amazon. But consider that they themselves weren't anything like their current forms ten years ago. Google started as a search engine, and Amazon.com started as an online book retailer. The power of openness is what made them international powerhouses.

Fight Against a Closed Mindset

Although we all like to think of ourselves as open-minded, flexible, adaptable people, we'd be smarter to admit to ourselves that this profile is rare. Human beings are excellent pattern recognizers, and leaders and successful businesspeople often achieve their roles by recognizing what has worked in the past, focusing on it, and excluding distractions.

The problem is that the world is changing rapidly, and so is what is working in and for organizations. An open mindset that leads to innovation and business model transformation is a wonderful adaptation in a fast-changing environment.

ASPIRE TO THESE TEN PRINCIPLES

NOW THAT YOU'VE REACHED THE LAST OF THE NETWORK PRINciples, let's take a minute to reflect where your company currently lies on the spectrum of each principle. We hope that the foregoing chapters have given you insight on where the most exciting companies are headed, why these transitions are important, and how they contribute to greater value—for your organization and for your networks. Even more, we hope that you've found inspiration—a few principles, or maybe even all ten, that you would be excited to enact with your team and in your businesses.

Before we describe the PIVOT process, where you start to shift your organization from firm-centric to network-centric, take a minute to step back and look at your profile on the ten principles. If you haven't done so already, map your current state on the image on the next page, "The ten principles." Then add your points to get a score between 10 (entirely firm-centric) and 100 (entirely network-centric). This is your starting point. We hope you'll revisit this score after working through PIVOT and see how far you have come. You can also see how your score compares to others and see the top performers by business model and industry at openmatters.com.

The ten principles

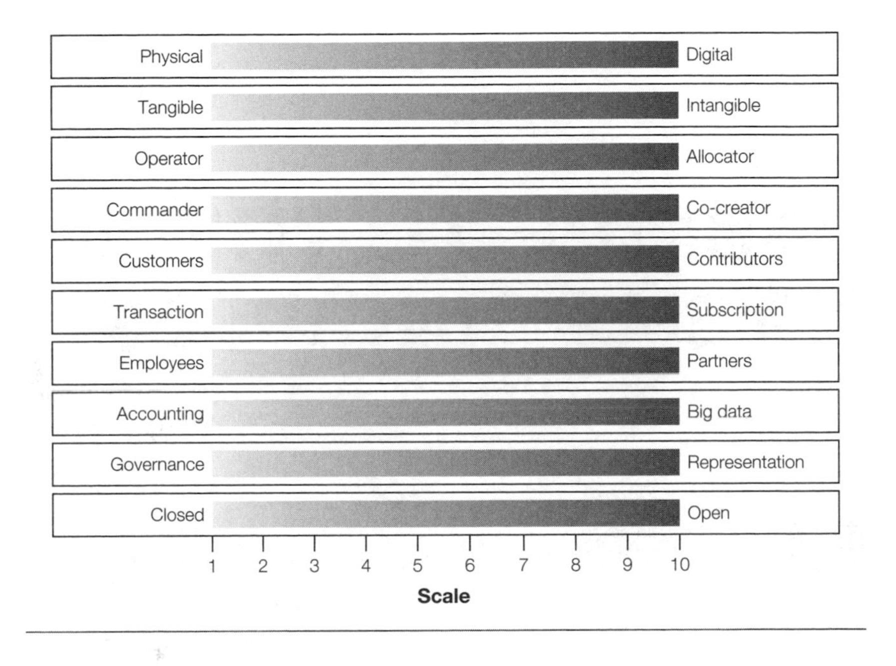

It's time to move from industry to platform, from closed to open, and ultimately from firm to network. The market is waiting for your network, so let's move on to the process you can use to create this exciting change.

THE PIVOT

PART THREE

Five Steps for Implementing Network Business Models

INTRODUCTION TO PIVOT

The digital revolution is different. It is akin to the economic body developing its neurological or sensory system, defining and refining its cognitive skills through investment in intellectual capital.

—Andy Haldane, chief economist, Bank of England

LEARNING IS ALWAYS A WORTHY ENDEAVOR, BUT IT DOES NO good unless you can figure out how to *implement* and *make useful* what you have learned. In part III of this book, we show you a practical process to implement network orchestration in your own organization.

Does that sound too ambitious? You're right. You're not going to transform your organization's business model this month, or even this year. Instead, you can plant a seed—select a network and create a platform where the network can both contribute and receive value, as can your organization. You will begin with a small network investment in a single portion of your business—one that has the potential to grow into a new core business. As you nurture, adapt, and grow this seed along the way, you will practice the asset allocation, business model, mental

The PIVOT process

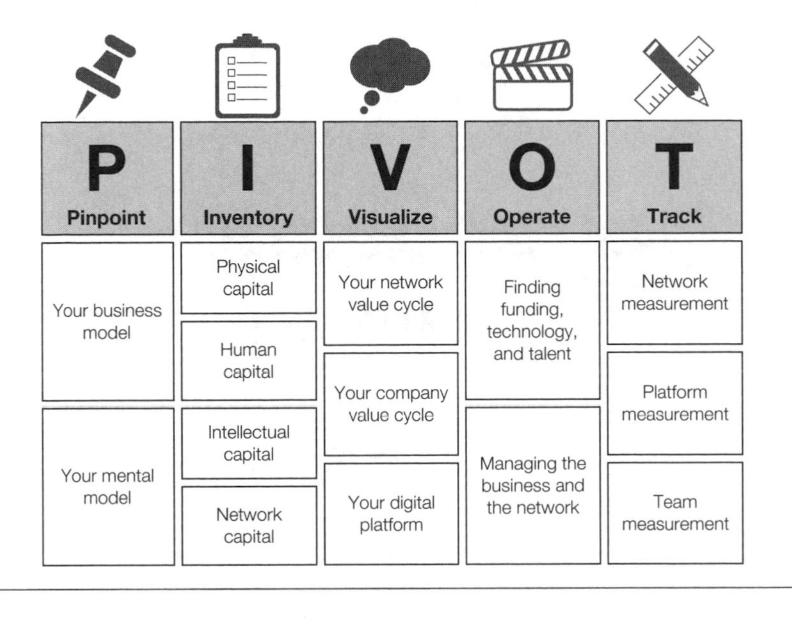

model, and leadership principles that differentiate network orchestrators from the pack, leading to happier customers, employees, and investors.

We've spent the past ten chapters discussing the great shifts that set network orchestrators apart and lead to their success. The great shifts, however, take place on the macro level, and it's not easy to implement macro-level change. For that reason, part III focuses on the micro level—five steps (Pinpoint, Inventory, Visualize, Operate, and Track, or PIVOT) to guide you through incremental changes and investments to set the stage for network growth. For each step we give straightforward guidance, bite-sized recommendations that you can implement as experiments and then iterate in your own organization, along with real-world examples of how other companies are adapting. We help you create a network that fits the capabilities of your organization.

Here are the five steps of PIVOT:

1. Pinpoint: Identify your current business model.

2. Inventory: Take stock of all your assets.

3. Visualize: Create your new network business model.

4. Operate: Enact your network business model.

5. Track: Measure what matters for a network business.

Each chapter opens by looking at how business model innovation is transforming an industry and then transitions into specific guidance for accomplishing the goals of each step in your own organization. We also include case studies that benchmark what network orchestration looks like in other organizations, both in start-ups and in established firms.

At the end of each chapter, we reflect on what each step looked like as we went through the PIVOT process with Enterprise Community Partners, Inc., a treasured client. Enterprise was one of the first organizations to use our fully developed PIVOT framework, and we are grateful for its courage and boldness and for allowing us to use its story of value creation through network orchestration as a case study in this book.

Jim Rouse and his wife, Patty Rouse, founded the not-for-profit in 1982 on a simple principle: to solve the problems facing low-income communities—from persistent poverty to poor health and educational outcomes—we must start by providing safe, healthy, and affordable homes. The Rouses saw housing as the critical "first rung on the ladder of opportunity."[1]

Over the next thirty-plus years, Enterprise has invested more than $18 billion and helped to build 340,000 affordable homes. But Enterprise is far more than a financial institution or public policy advocate. It is in the business of helping create opportunity for people by building networks—with home at the center.

Digital technologies have created new opportunities to connect people and create opportunity for low- and moderate-income families to raise their standard of living. Digital networks are fast becoming an integral part of life for even the poorest in the world, as you saw in the refugee story presented earlier in this book.

Terri Ludwig, Enterprise CEO, sees the opportunity to expand the organization's impact on its target group by leveraging digital technologies. Although housing is the first rung of need, Ludwig says that the firm can go much further, connecting individuals to education, jobs, health, and other foundational building blocks of opportunity.

Enterprise has begun exploring how it could use big data analytics and technology-enabled social and mobile networks to serve its mission. Its leaders are asking new, *what if* questions that are changing both how they think and what they do:

- What if we knew more about the lives of residents in Enterprise-supported homes?
- What if we knew more about their unique needs, from the health needs of a senior to the educational gaps of a child?
- What if we knew more about the emerging trends in their cities and neighborhoods?

Enterprise's leadership team, with the authors' help, has been tackling a significant transformation as it seeks to apply PIVOT to its business model, from financial services and local program development and policy, to a new, digitally enabled direction. Ludwig's overarching objective for Enterprise is to fulfill Jim Rouse's original vision: to help solve the toughest, most intractable problems facing low-income communities and to be a "light to show the way."

We return to the Enterprise story throughout this PIVOT section to show you how this transformation is taking place in one organization. We hope it will provide guidance and inspiration.

Note that additional resources and support can also be found at openmatters.com.

PINPOINT

Identify Your Current Business Model

Silicon Valley is coming.
There are hundreds of start-ups with a lot of brains and money working on various alternatives to traditional banking.

—Jamie Dimon, CEO, JPMorgan Chase

RETAIL BANKING IS CHANGING. MORE THAN HALF (51 PERCENT) OF banking executives surveyed by *Business Insider* predicted that financial technology (fintech) disruptors would see the most success in retail banking, including areas such as depositing savings, managing transactions, and providing loans.[1] Major consumer banks expect retail banking to plummet from 35 percent of revenues to only 16 percent by 2020.

What is happening? Network business models are engulfing financial services just as in other industries. In short, fintech start-ups are allowing banking customers to serve themselves, and each other, in novel ways. Rather than get cash or write a check to pay one's share of the rent, the connected banking consumer can use PayPal or Venmo. When it

comes to savings accounts, millennials are turning to digital-only banks such as Fidor, companies that go as far as to provide outside developers with APIs (application programming interfaces), which give developers tools to interface with the banks' software source code to let them innovate the banks' platforms. Those in need of loans can crowd-source via Kickstarter or Lending Club. This trend is even moving beyond the individual. Many small businesses have turned to Square or ApplePay to take credit and debit card payments.

The rise of network orchestration as a business model for financial services has led to great opportunities for customer self-service, peer-to-peer interaction, and collective collaboration. Whereas old banks were focused on having skilled employees serve their customers—often using brick-and-mortar retail outlets, ATMs, or call centers—innovative financial service providers now allow customers and investors to serve, save, and invest for themselves via the digital platforms (such as Wealthfront, a personalized investment management app; or Charles Schwab's Intelligent Portfolio service) to meet our individual needs.

As a result, well-established banks and financial services firms are facing a gargantuan question. How can they transform themselves from service providers to network orchestrators? Although the established players have the advantage of brand and installed customer bases, upstart and well-capitalized digital innovators are unburdened by cumbersome organizations, politics, historical inertia, and institutional memory. Only time will tell, but the most self-aware banks have already begun innovating, incubating, partnering, and adapting.

PIVOT Step 1: Pinpoint

The goal of the Pinpoint step, which often takes up to one month, is to identify your current business model as well as your current mental model: the preferences, biases, and decisions that have gotten you where you are and keep you there. To decide whether you will join the digitally networked world and how you will get there, you must fully accept and

appreciate your starting place. Once you understand your current state, whether asset builder, service provider, or technology creator, you will be able to create a new, more valuable network vision for your future.

Beginning to Pinpoint Your Business Model

The story of your value, growth, and profit begins with an assessment of your current business model. The key insight of our research is that the four business models have dramatically different growth rates, profit margins, and valuations. However, very few companies take advantage of the most valuable business model—network orchestration. This means that there is a great value gap for boards and leaders to close, and that's probably why you're reading this book.

Because your business model follows from the mental models and investment decisions of the leadership team, we suggest that you conduct the Pinpoint step with your executive team or with peer leaders, whatever your level. A group of six to eight executives is about the right size to represent a diverse set of skills (marketing, sales, technology, finance, operations, etc.) but still be able to reach a consensus. It's important to include all major functions, and it's crucial to have someone from the finance function so that you can examine your capital allocation and compare your organization's performance on key metrics to business model averages. Once this core team develops a viewpoint on the business model, it should be shared for feedback with the board and the management team.

If the team does preparatory reading on business models (i.e., this book), you can begin pinpointing in a one-day offsite. As prereading, we suggest reviewing OpenMatters' *Harvard Business Review* articles on business models and browsing the tools and information available on openmatters.com.[2]

Here's a caveat, however: often, reflection over time deepens understanding of business models, as well as their relationship to leaders' mental models, which include attitudes, assumptions, and biases. Most individuals find that once they internalize their business model, they can spot myriad ways that the organization focuses on and invests in

one model and one type of asset, neglecting the others. Often, holding a second offsite two to four weeks after the first meeting yields deeper, more valuable insights on business and mental models.

Note, too, that although you can transform your network only through the integrated efforts of a team, it must be initiated by a single motivated individual. This change leader could be at any level in the firm, but she will need the support of the CEO and the board—the true decision makers about capital allocation. If this mission inspires you, be prepared to personally shepherd your organization's transformation to network orchestration, and represent it to the executive team and board. Although you don't need to be tactically involved in each step in PIVOT, you will need to lead and guide the teams.

Defining Your Current Business Model

As a reminder, the four business models are asset builders, service providers, technology creators, and network orchestrators. Each business model is based, respectively, on a different type of asset: physical capital, human capital, intellectual capital, and network capital.

Business models and multipliers

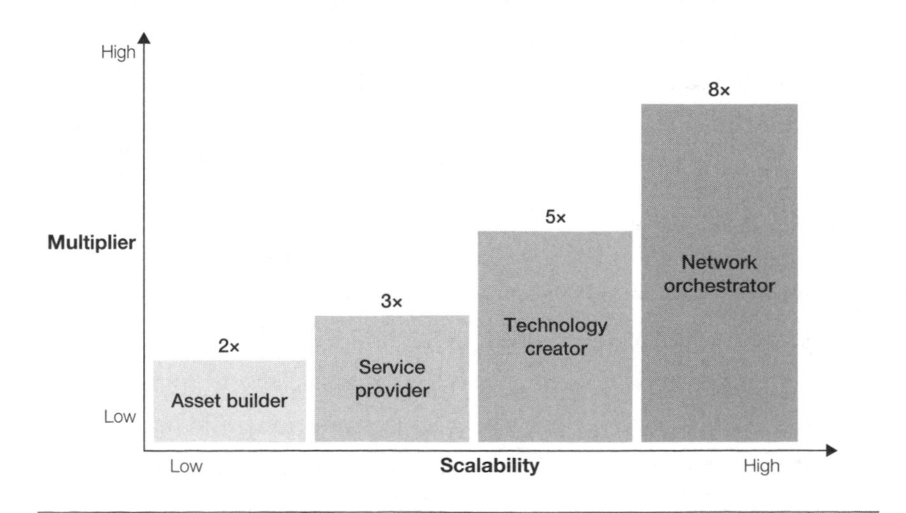

- *Asset builders* deliver value through physical goods. These companies make, market, distribute, sell, and lease things. Examples include Ford, Walmart, and American Airlines.
- *Service providers* deliver value through people. These companies hire skilled workers who provide services to customers for which they charge. Examples include United Healthcare, Accenture, and JPMorgan Chase.
- *Technology creators* deliver value through ideas. These companies develop and sell intellectual property such as software, analytics, pharmaceuticals, and biotechnology. Examples include Microsoft, Oracle, and Amgen.
- *Network orchestrators* deliver value through connectivity. These companies create a platform where participants interact or transact with the many other members of the network. They may sell products, build relationships, share advice, give reviews, collaborate, and more. Examples include eBay, Red Hat, and Visa.

Pinpointing your business model can be surprisingly tricky. Although you and your team probably have some intuition about what your company's primary business model is, many leaders focus on their industry designations. Our research indicates this approach isn't very useful, given that all four business models can operate in any industry. In addition, many companies operate several business models simultaneously. But each company in the S&P 1500 had a primary business model that was the focus of its investments and efforts. Therefore, we approach this issue by considering specific questions regarding the characteristics of your organization and its economic performance.

Identifying Your Organization's Characteristics

Companies with different business models look different in a number of ways—from capital investment to time management to metrics and reports. Let's begin exploring your firm's characteristics with a simple business

model audit. Have each member of your Pinpoint team answer these questions, and be sure to discuss any points of disagreement. In the end, you will determine which primary business model your firm best matches.

1. Which of the following descriptions best describes your organization?

    A. Manufacturer, distributor, or retailer

    B. Professional services, care provider, or consultancy

    C. Developer or creator of technology, biotechnology, or pharmaceuticals

    D. Platform provider, facilitator, or connector

2. Where does the bulk of your allocated capital go?

    A. Property, plant, and equipment (PPE)

    B. Payroll for employees who provide services to customers

    C. Research and development for software, patents, and other IP

    D. Building and evangelizing a network or platform

3. What does top talent usually do at your firm?

    A. Plant, production, and operations

    B. Client or customer services

    C. Research and development

    D. Digital development (cloud, big data analytics, social, and mobile)

4. What risks are of greatest concern to your organization?

    A. Damage to PPE, loss of inventory

    B. Loss of key employees

C. Inability to protect your IP (pirated software, generic drugs, etc.)

D. Loss or declining loyalty of customers

5. Which of the following activities is most important for the competitive success of your organization?

   A. Efficient manufacturing, distribution, and operations

   B. Hiring the right talent and keeping utilization up

   C. Protecting IP and developing new technologies

   D. Creating customer interactions and tapping in to the crowd

6. What KPIs are the most important for leaders to track in your firm?

   A. Inventory turnover, production efficiency

   B. Hours billed, employee utilization

   C. R&D output, creation of new IP (patents, software, biotech)

   D. Visitors, users, subscriptions, and transactions

(You can also take this survey online at openmatters.com.) In the foregoing questions, each letter is associated with a type of business model. *A* responses indicate an asset builder business model; *B* responses, service provider; *C* responses, technology creator; and *D* responses, network orchestrator.

Look at the distribution of your lettered answers to determine the primary business model indicated by your firm's characteristics. It's likely your answers will not align completely with a single business model. Most firms employ a mix of models but do have one that predominates.

Reviewing Your Firm's Economic Performance

Next, consider the financial and operational performance of your firm. Do you perform like a network orchestrator or an asset builder?

Business model performance

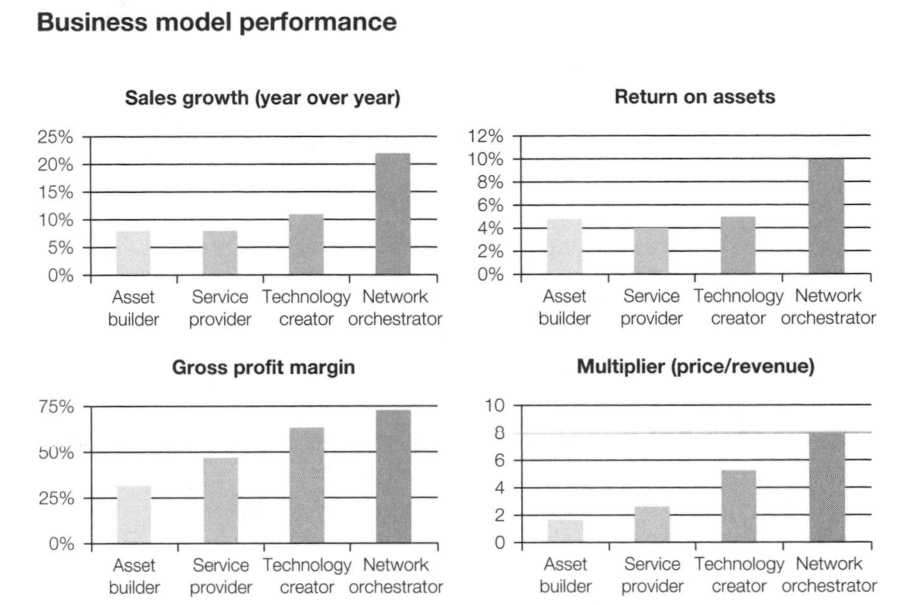

Our research identified several key metrics for which companies with different business models have differentiated performance. Let's look at the average performance, by business model, on four key metrics: sales growth, return on assets, gross profit margin, and multiplier (price-to-revenue ratio).

Gather these numbers from your finance representative, and look at where your company falls on the charts in the figure above. Which business model does your economic performance best match?

Bringing It All Together

At this point, you've looked at business models from two directions, and you probably have already reached a conclusion about your company's. It's useful to bring your team's intuitions to this problem as well, but if the team's intuitions go against the data in the preceding two thought exercises, the intuitions may be leading you astray. The business models

of most companies are less valuable than leaders like to believe, and their multipliers betray the truth. Nearly nine out of ten companies are asset builders or service providers, which perform comparatively poorly in all four metrics.

You may feel that your organization falls within a few business models, and this can certainly be true. Perhaps you are 70 percent asset builder and 30 percent service provider. That's fine, but it's worth your time to decide which business model is the *focus* of your company.

Wherever you are—and for most firms, that will be asset builder—tackling the thinking and processes in this book will help you shift from firm-centric (which describes asset builders, service providers, and technology creators) to network-centric and to achieve a significant competitive advantage in growth, profits, and marginal costs.

Pinpoint Your Mental Model

If you want to do something about your business model, you will also need to understand *why* it is your business model. There are reasons your firm chooses certain assets for investments, and those reasons are based on the mental models of your leadership team.

The average CEO is fifty-six years old.[3] This means that he was already an adult when ARPANET (the nascent internet) was just taking off—and well over forty when Facebook was founded.

Most business leaders were educated, trained, and began work in a time when physical assets dominated the markets and the best leaders were operational and finance experts. For most leaders, their thinking and skill sets have not changed significantly in the past twenty years, while over that same period, new technologies have proliferated, new types of assets have taken prominence, and customers and employees have become empowered. These changes create a gap in values as well as skills.

Skills are important because all of us are most comfortable working in areas where we consider ourselves capable, if not expert. Each person on the team should think about the following questions:

- What has your education and experience prepared you for?
- Which of the four asset types do you prefer (believe will deliver reward versus risk)?
- What about the team around you? Do they have similar skills and experiences? Do you reinforce or challenge each other's mental models?

Values are even harder to change than skills. We develop values at a formative time in our lives, mostly unconsciously, and sadly we rarely revisit or change them. To consider your values, it's helpful to start by reflecting on how you think about the four types of assets:

- Physical assets such as factories, stores, products, and inventory
- Human assets such as skilled workers and customers
- Intellectual capital assets such as R&D, patents, and software
- Network assets such as relationships and platforms

In your Pinpoint team, answer these questions:

- Which asset do you believe brings the most risk to a firm?
- Which asset is the most difficult to manage?
- Which asset generates the most value?
- What types of assets do the most valuable firms have?
- What is the most important asset for your organization?

(You can take the assessment online at openmatters.com.)

Your beliefs about these questions drive how your firm spends and makes money and how you create value—but they may be based on

assumptions, biases, or outdated information. If it were your job to argue against yourself, could you provide some good counterpoints?

For example, many executives think that network assets are difficult to understand, quantify, manage, and measure. After all, these assets exist outside the organization and are not traditional assets, as measured by accounting, nor are they put into the records of the organization. On the other hand, networks may be the easiest asset to manage, because at their best they are actually self-managed by the community, as you have seen in earlier chapters. For example, when a new vacation hot spot becomes popular, Airbnb's network of hosts begins expanding into that area on their own—in the best interests of both the network and the company.

Remember that we're shifting from a world of tangible, physical assets to intangible, digital assets, and from owned to shared. These assets scale faster and more cost-effectively than physical, owned assets and have the ability to grow and manage themselves. However, you can't manage them in the way you manage owned production plants, coffeepots, employees, or intellectual property. A new mental model is a necessity for success in the network world, and we will discuss adapting mental models further in part IV.

The First PIVOT Step Is the Hardest

Reflecting on your current business and mental models, with the ultimate purpose of changing them, is a difficult task. Familiar assets and familiar thinking are comfortable, and we certainly hope that you're fond of your company just as it is. But ongoing success requires ongoing adaptation. There is enormous potential in front of you, and we hope it is inspiring and exciting.

Pinpointing your business model gives you your starting point. Let's consider it a launching pad. As we keep going with PIVOT, we get increasingly practical about what you're launching toward and how you're going to get there.

The Enterprise Pinpoint Story

When we began working with Enterprise, it integrated policy, services, and finance, but it was on the left side on most of the ten principles in the from-to spectra. The team members focused on financing low- and moderate-income housing (physical, tangible assets), but they knew very little about the residents of their financed buildings, their twenty-five hundred real estate developer partners, or their supply chain of contractors and service firms. The Enterprise team members had no technology that enabled them to get input from those they served nor to understand the organization's impact on clients' lives either directly or indirectly (through partners), let alone co-create with them. However, the team members were willing to admit this to themselves and commit to transformation.

Pradip Sitaram, Enterprise's chief information officer (CIO), was a key player in prompting its technology transformation—essentially seeking to disrupt its traditional beliefs and operations. Sitaram, who joined the leadership team in 2010, had begun implementing a cloud platform to improve the organization's operations, but he also saw the potential in using digital networks to further the organization's true mission of bringing *opportunity* to low-income families and children. Luckily he had a partner in Charlie Werhane, president of the organization, and Craig Mellendick, chief financial officer. Werhane, Mellendick, and Sitaram knew that technology could be a differentiator for Enterprise and that they needed to invest in it if they wanted to think and operate differently from their competitors.

Werhane knew that there was great promise in bringing digital technology to the firm, but over time he realized that the real opportunity was to turn the firm into a network orchestrator, with the partners and residents as its center. To get there, he needed the support of the board. Terri Ludwig wanted Enterprise's impact on low- and moderate-income families and children to go far beyond housing, to include a network of services, such as health care, education, transportation, and even microfinancing, to be delivered digitally to help improve their lives.

But the organization had far to go to migrate from an asset builder and financial services firm to a digitally enabled network orchestrator. Even its aspirational goal—stated as "solving housing insecurity"—was limiting in its focus on physical assets. Enterprise had no technologists on its board, and although it was good at financing housing and providing needed services to the local community, it had little information on what its actual impact was or whom it was really serving.

To increase its impact, Ludwig called together the executive team members for an intense two-day offsite to discuss how they might pivot the business. During the meeting, the executives worked to pinpoint their individual mental models, and the resulting people, processes, and practices, that kept them focused on building assets and providing services. They reflected on how digital technologies could greatly increase their impact on the market, including public policy in Washington, DC, where they had great sway, having financed more than 340,000 housing units with $18 billion in capital.

With the starting place identified, they felt ready to start identifying all the assets (tangible and intangible) they had at their disposal. They knew it wouldn't be an easy task, but they all agreed it was worth the effort. Next, we turn to the step of inventorying your assets.

INVENTORY

Take Stock of All Your Assets

What's dangerous is not to evolve.

—Jeff Bezos, CEO, Amazon.com

RETAIL IS CHANGING. IN MANY US CITIES, AMAZON NOW DELIVers Double Stuf Oreos (or whatever else you currently need) to your door in less than two hours, while allowing you to track the product from shelf to door. This is an amazing feat for a company that didn't exist twenty years ago, in an industry—internet retailing—that barely existed before its arrival. Amazon is even beginning to experiment with a crowd-sourced delivery service.

Networks and digital technologies have influenced retail in many ways. Most major retailers develop relationships with bloggers and sponsor posts that advertise their goods. They often maintain a significant presence on all major social media platforms (Starbucks has more than a million followers on Instagram—pretty good for a coffee company), and they use big data analytics to learn about and better serve their customers.

You might think that the whole world is moving online and to the digital network and that brick-and-mortar is going the way of the

dinosaurs, but some traditional retailers have found that their physical assets can be used to complement their emerging technology and network business models. Macy's and Walmart, along with several others, have become masters of omnichannel strategies. Their customers can shop at home, in stores, or even on their phones and receive the product through delivery or in-store pickup—whichever is most convenient. Although the use of physical assets (stores, warehouses, and distribution centers) is shifting, innovative retailers use every possible means to relate to and serve customers compared with strictly online or offline retailers. It goes to show that the digital network revolution can complement and bolster traditional asset builders and service providers.

The next step in the PIVOT process, Inventory, is about figuring out what your company has (across all asset categories, even ones you might not currently consider assets) and can use to help build and strengthen a network business model.

PIVOT Step 2: Inventory

The goal of the Inventory step, which typically takes one to two months, is to create a complete inventory of the assets in your organization, considering each of the four asset types. We focus on those assets that historically have not been carefully assessed or managed: intangible assets such as intellectual capital and relationships. Because highly scalable network business models usually utilize digital technologies, you will also assess your firm's digital capability.

Building a new business model within a portion of your existing operation means reallocating some of your capital to a different mix of assets. Most organizations know very well what their physical, tangible assets are. They carefully track revenues, cash, inventory, property, plant, and equipment. In contrast, intangible assets, such as human and intellectual capital, usually get less focus. Your company probably has a portfolio of intangible assets, but it's likely you don't fully utilize, activate, measure, or, in some cases, even view them as assets. In this step,

you will review these assets to identify the most promising place to build a new network initiative.

Understanding your complete, current asset base will help you understand your organization's focus and main capabilities, as well as identify gaps and opportunities. The Inventory step will help you determine what you have and what you need to build or acquire in order to create a network initiative.

Beginning to Inventory Your Assets

We examine each asset type in turn. As a reminder, here are the four types:

- *Physical capital:* tangible assets including cash, plant, property, and equipment
- *Human capital:* skilled and capable employees, teams, and alumni
- *Intellectual capital:* software, biotechnology, and patents
- *Network capital:* relationships, interactions, connectivity, and associated insights

To complete a thorough inventory will require a team larger than just you and this book. Although your knowledge as a leader will help fill in many of the boxes, we recommend building out a multifunction task force; include subject matter experts in each part of your organization, such as all major product lines, marketing, human resources, and legal. The key is to make sure your team represents the full variety of your assets.

Each member of the task force is responsible for cataloging the four types of assets within a subset of the company's operations. To start this process, all task force members should gather for a kickoff meeting to review the specifics related to each asset type discussed in this chapter. Any areas of overlap should be carefully addressed to avoid redundant efforts and wasted time.

Once the task force members are up to speed, they're ready to go out into the organization and sit down with leaders and managers to discuss the asset types within their domains. These meetings can usually be accomplished over the course of a month and should cover the assets, their descriptions, and value where appropriate. The finished work product for each member of the task force includes two or three pages for each of the four asset types, with a list and high-level description of the key assets in that category.

To help you with this process, we have listed all the asset types. These lists are not complete, but they act as a starting point for understanding your asset base and discovering what you will need to grow into a network orchestrator.

Part of the process is to choose your task force carefully. The right members will have ready expertise in the areas they are inventorying, as

The asset inventory

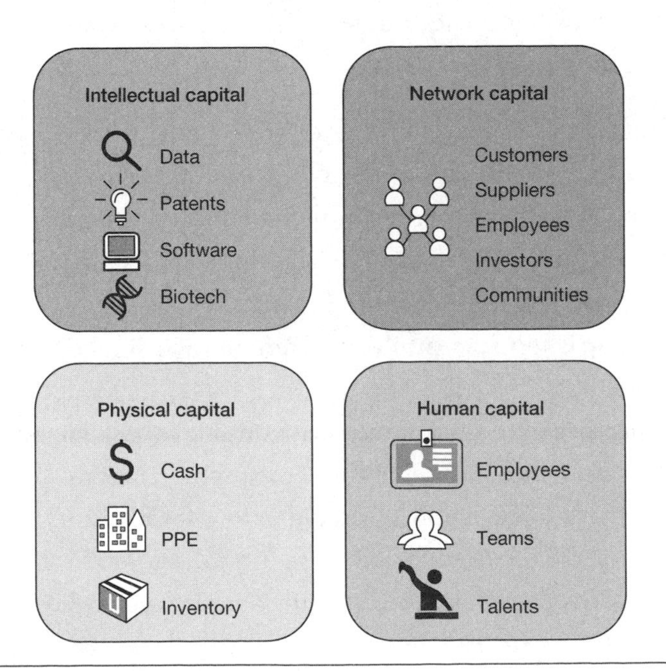

well as an interest in the network project. The interviews they hold are good opportunities to increase buy-in and gain perspective from leaders around the company.

When the inventories of all assets are complete, they should be presented to the leadership team, usually the same team that did the Pinpoint step. During this day of presentations, you should spend significant time assessing the affinities, attributes, and potentials of each network. Deep understanding of your networks is essential for success in the following PIVOT steps. At the end, you will have a complete view of all the assets existing in your company, even intangibles, and you will be ready to design a new business model.

Inventorying Physical Capital Assets

You will start your inventory with the easy one: physical assets. Together, your task force will create a list of your firm's tangible, physical assets. Categories to consider include cash, property, plants, equipment, and inventory. Add as much detail as you can, and values when available, but don't spend more than a week on this. Much of the information should be detailed in your organization's financial reports.

You might ask, Why even bother with physical assets when the goal is to shift toward a network business? One simple reason is that you need to understand what funds you have available that can be invested in a new endeavor. Second, physical assets can complement a network business model. For example, a Nest thermostat both gathers data and uses the data to better serve its network of users. Amazon uses its distribution centers to allow other sellers to sell and ship through the Amazon platform. And a complete inventory, including all asset types, will sharpen your view of your current asset portfolio and reveal how much attention and capital you spend on each type.

Inventorying Human Capital Assets

Next, your team will examine the human capital assets in your workforce. Begin by thinking about the various groups of employees, or contractors,

that work for your organization. You can organize your thoughts in any way that makes sense to you, perhaps using an organizational chart or categorizing according to product lines, geographies, and the like.

For each employee group, identify the key skills or talents that differentiate it from others within and outside the firm. For example, your engineer groups may specialize in various technologies specific to your products. Take note of employees as well as teams that have special profiles, unique skill sets, or experience that make them difficult to replace.

Pay careful attention to technological capability during the human capital assessment. Recall that several digital technologies—social, mobile, cloud, big data analytics, and the internet of things—are closely associated with the network orchestrator business model. Note carefully how you currently leverage each of these technologies, if at all, and what level of expertise your employees and contractors have. This question has implications at all levels; not only do you need the hands-on skills to create and manage the technology, but you also need the thought leadership on your management team and board to conceive and support the projects.

Finding the right talent is just as key for network orchestrators as for any other company with any other business model, and the hunt for digital talent is becoming increasingly competitive. The trend of *acqui-hiring*, or acquiring a company solely for the purpose of bringing in its talent, has grown in Silicon Valley over the past few years, with Facebook, Twitter, Yahoo!, and Google leading the way.

The purpose of assessing your human capital assets is to gauge your staff members' ability to create a digital platform to support a network business, and also to determine whether they possess knowledge or could provide services that would attract and provide value to a network. For example, staff software designers could collaborate with the network on software development or coach those wishing to enter the field.

Inventorying Intellectual Capital Assets

The third asset the task force will examine is intellectual capital—assets that are based on ideas and information. One important aspect of

intellectual capital is the data your firm owns or can access. Data takes many forms and is often scattered throughout the organization. There may be data that you have actively sought to gain, such as hiring an external firm to do market research on your key customer segments, or data that you collect during the course of operations. Operational data can come from in-store or online transactions, website visits, manufacturing processes, and many other sources. Consider, as well, the data you *could* collect but do not do so currently.

Other categories of note are patents, biotechnology, trade secrets, trademarks, copyrights, brands, logos, and software, whether sold as a product or created for internal use.

The key question to think about is, "What do we know that is unique, differentiated, and potentially of interest to our networks?" Remember that in a network orchestrator business model, both the network and the company provide value. You examine intellectual capital assets in order to understand what knowledge you have that might be of interest to your network—whether you share it, collaborate on it, or sell it.

Inventorying Network Capital Assets

The last, but probably most important, category to inventory is your network capital. Begin by listing all of your organization's key networks. There will be some that you manage closely, and others that you barely interact with. Consider the following categories, but note that there may be multiple, unique networks within each category. For example, you may have several distinct customer groups with different characteristics.

- Customers
- Prospects
- Employees
- Alumni
- Suppliers
- Distributors

- Integrators
- Investors
- Communities
- Peers
- Competitors

When you have a complete list of your networks, you then review the characteristics of each one. First, consider the level of affinity between members of the network and your company: is it high, medium, or low? You could think about network members' general sentiment, their frequency of interaction, and their satisfaction with your organization and its products.

Second, think about what each party gets from the relationship. For example, at the simplest level, customers receive products, and companies receive money through their relationship. With many network organizations, however, customers receive esteem or shared revenues, and the companies benefit from customers' ideas and insights. When you think about the benefits each group receives, remember the four asset types. Benefits can include physical things like goods and products; services provided by people; information and ideas; or relationships such as network access.

Finally, consider the potential of each relationship. Each network may have other assets and abilities that could be valuable to you. Likewise, the organization may have additional information, services, or relationships that the network would find useful, interesting, or valuable. We use the tool in the figure on the next page to assess networks with our clients.

It's important to spend adequate time and effort in inventorying your networks. Most firms have never before taken this approach to understanding their networks, and doing it well may require additional meetings with various teams in your company, or even reaching out to the networks themselves.

Developing and expanding network capital is the foundation of network orchestration. Most network assets go underrecognized and

The network asset inventory tool

	General		Current state of relationship		Potential future relationship	
Network	Description	Affinity level	What the network gets	What the company gets	What the network wants	What the organization wants

underutilized. Networks store a vast array of talents, skills, and assets but are rarely activated to share value with companies. By cataloging the networks that exist in and around your firm, you're preparing for the next step: creating a new network-centered business model.

There Will Be Gaps

The inventory process is long and detailed, but it truly shows you what you have to work with and identifies any gaps in your portfolio. For most firms, the inventory process reinforces the impact of their business model—few highly cultivated network assets and low capability with key digital technologies, but a lot of physical capital assets.

Don't be discouraged. You have what it takes to apply the PIVOT process to your organization; you only need to cultivate some of the assets you have largely been ignoring and invest in some of the technologies and talent that you used to think weren't relevant to your industry or core business. Completing your inventory sets the stage for you to understand exactly where you are currently and to visualize a new, exciting, and value-generating business model for your firm. That's the next step.

The Enterprise Inventory Story

After realizing that their business and mental models were grounded firmly in physical assets and local services that were delivered by partners, Enterprise leaders began to take stock of the intangible assets they had with which they could begin to build a technology-enabled network for their key stakeholders. The executives also began to think about how Enterprise could extend the cloud-based technology platform that CIO Pradip Sitaram and his team had built over the prior five years. They also were ready to determine how the platform could be used to create a business-to-business digital network in the asset management, loan origination, and resident management arenas of the nonprofit.

CFO Craig Mellendick worked hard to assemble the firm's complete tangible and intangible asset inventory, considering the four asset types. This was difficult work, given that the firm, in its thirty-year history, had not created a system to track or measure its intangible assets.

Many of the intangible assets that they would need to leverage were not clear to the team members. To move toward digital networks, the organization created a task force of its executive team plus a number of business analysts to measure its nonphysical assets:

- Network assets such as its suppliers and residents
- Intellectual assets such as brand and best practices
- Human assets such as people, partners, and contractors

As the Enterprise team learned about the PIVOT process, they found it remarkable how little information the organization had on an important network: the families that lived in the communities it had financed. Based on its history and business model, Enterprise carefully tracked and reported on the amount invested and the number of units built, as well as the services and public policy programs that were financed—but Mellendick discovered that no one in the organization could tell you about the people that Enterprise ultimately served.

In preparing for the fall board meeting, the leadership team learned that this key network—the one that the Enterprise mission was to serve and create opportunities for—had almost no affinity with the organization and that there was no technology in place to serve the members. Likewise, Enterprise knew very little about these families—how satisfied they were and how their communities could better meet their needs. Both the leadership team and the board agreed that there was untapped potential in their networks, and they began to create a vision for an exciting transformation.

VISUALIZE

Create Your New Network Business Model

We view ourselves both as an automotive company, and as a mobility company.

—Mark Fields, CEO, Ford Motor Company

VISUALIZING YOUR ORGANIZATION AS A DIGITAL NETWORK, even in a small portion of the business, is a similar leap to the one made fifteen or more years ago by every great leader telling her teams and boards, "We need to get our organization online." Most people did not know what that meant, but the best made the leap.

To be sure, every industry is undergoing a change, including those grounded in physical assets—transportation and lodging. You've heard of Uber, and probably Lyft, and maybe even their car-sharing grandparent Zipcar—not to mention Getaround, RelayRides, Greenwheels, GoCar, and many more. Car sharing and driving-as-a-service are available in more than a thousand cities around the world. The accessibility and convenience of these options are a threat to the car industry as well as the taxi and limousine industries, as millennials seem happy to get around without either a driver's license or car ownership.

Travelers now have options that extend far beyond standard hotel rooms. You've likely heard of Airbnb, Homeaway, and VRBO (vacation rental by owner). These are similar network-based businesses, but for homes and bedrooms instead of cars. Through these network-based listing services, you can now rent a home, a bedroom, or even space for a tent in someone's yard. Although hoteliers like to say that these services address a different market than standard hotel customers, there is no denying that the lodging revolution has hit hotels' bottom lines.

One of the major advantages of network lodging options is that they can rapidly scale up and down. Major hotel chains have noticed that their ability to charge very high rates for "tent pole" events, such as a major music festival or a visit from the pope, have declined as enterprising local residents list their guest bedrooms on Airbnb to capitalize on spikes in demand.

What has happened? Technology allows owners to increase the utilization of some of their most expensive assets: their cars and their homes. Around the world, millions of car owners have paid to buy, fuel, insure, and maintain their cars while using them only an hour or so per day. Homeowners frequently have extra space in guest rooms and basements that is rarely utilized. Network innovators have broken down historical barriers, such as the need for licensing and the difficulty of finding customers, to enable a new source of revenue generation.

Technology is now catching up to travelers' needs and desires and is allowing a broader population a share in the value creation by using cloud platforms and mobile technology.

PIVOT Step 3: Visualize

The goal of the Visualize step, which takes one to two months, is to design an inspiring network-based business that will begin to help your company apply PIVOT to at least a portion of its capital, time, and talent, turning to network orchestration and starting to generate the increased value that this business model offers. Although we recommend starting

small, you should aim to find something that could, one day, grow into a significant portion of your business.

In this step, you design a new business initiative using the network orchestration business model. To do so, you will identify one network to activate; determine the value that the network, and your organization, will give and receive; and identify the platform and technology necessary to make it happen.

Beginning to Visualize Your Network

In this step, you will begin to get practical about creating a new future for your firm. You have already identified your firm's starting point—your business model, along with the many types of assets that you currently have at your disposal. In the Visualize step, you begin to put these components together in a meaningful way, creating a plan for reallocating your capital to scalable and low-cost assets and digital technologies. We

The network orchestrator business model

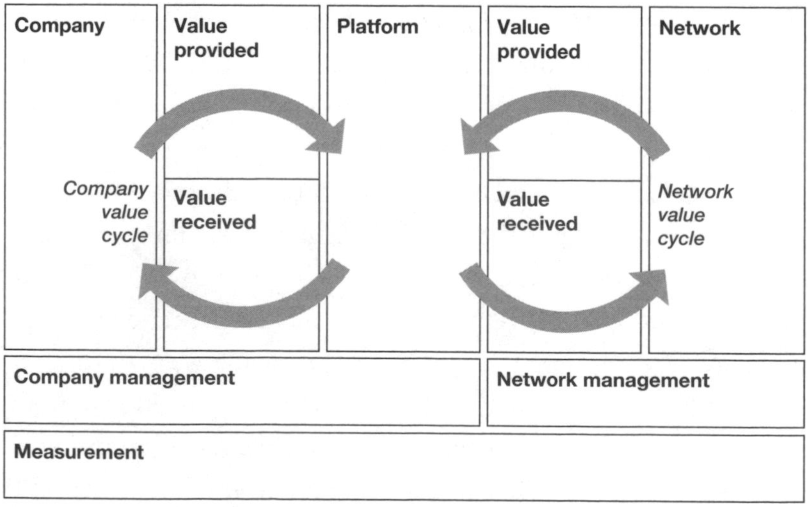

Company
Value provided
Platform
Value provided
Network
Company value cycle
Value received
Value received
Network value cycle
Company management
Network management
Measurement

will walk you through this step methodically, considering each component necessary for a network orchestration business model, the assets you have to work with, and the tools you will need.

In short, this step is like visualizing a new investment portfolio.

But first, let's break down network orchestration so that you can think carefully about each element. The network orchestrator business model diagram notes all the essential elements of a network business. As you can see, in network orchestration there is a value cycle for the company and a value cycle for the network, which intersect on a digital platform. The network, the company, and the platform are the key components you will focus on.

Note: you must also think carefully about managing your network (growing it and ensuring loyalty) and managing the internal side of the business (using the right management practices and iterative approach). We cover these management items, and complete the diagram for your organization, in the next chapter.

Gaining an Overview of the Process

You apply the Visualize step with a small team of leaders, all of whom have bought in to the process and are up-to-date on the previous steps. This is often the same group of leaders who undertook pinpointing your business model. Designing a new business, with a new business model, is a daunting undertaking, so we want to reassure you that you won't get it right the first time. Don't put that expectation on yourself or your team. Instead, we recommend you use an iterative process: the team creates a draft, shows it to experts in the organization for feedback, and then revisits and revises the draft.

The idea is to go through the Visualize step quickly and then repeat with more care and more insight. Giving people a week to digest the new ideas between iterations will greatly increase the effectiveness of your next meeting. As the team homes in on the most promising network possibilities, you can add experts to the team to help finalize the structure and create an implementation plan in the next step (Operate).

At the beginning, your team should feel free to try unexpected combinations, push the boundaries, and genuinely experiment. When people step out of comfortable business and mental models, everything may seem outlandish at first. Give your team time to sit with the ideas, iterate on them, and begin to see a new future.

Identifying Potential Networks

You will begin by focusing on the network. Because network trust, intimacy, and reciprocity (co-creation and shared economics) are the hallmarks of network orchestration, it makes sense to begin with a network focus.

To select a network to focus on, you begin by referring to your network inventory from the Inventory step, where you detailed your firm's many networks and their characteristics. Peruse your list of networks and focus on the key, and currently underserved, desires of each network as it relates to your company, products, or industry. You are looking for occasions when the network members could actually *serve their own* needs and wants, if properly enabled. As a business model, network orchestration is highly differentiated because it is the only model in which the company enables and allows the network to serve itself (participants serving other participants) instead of the company trying to serve all the network's needs on its own.

As you consider each network's needs, keep in mind the four asset classes. Network platforms can help facilitate the creation and exchange of any of the four types:

- Physical capital: access to physical assets that are related to your products, value proposition, or industry. Examples: Airbnb, Uber
- Human capital: expertise related to your products, processes, or industry. Examples: TaskRabbit, Apple Developer Network
- Intellectual capital: feedback on products or services, input on product design, data about themselves, or product usage. Examples: Yelp, TripAdvisor

- Network capital: word-of-mouth advertising, access to friends and family. Examples: Facebook, LinkedIn

The best place to begin is with those networks that already have high affinity for your firm; these members are the most likely to participate in a new network initiative. For each of your three to five top networks, create a list of the members' unmet needs and ways that the network might be able to serve its own needs.

Don't feel that you must get this right on the first try. You probably won't. Iteration is a necessary part of the process.

Analyzing Your Contribution

After selecting your top network opportunities, you consider the complementary piece: the value your firm can return to the network. You probably won't be able to finalize your thinking on network self-service before you move on. Again, this is an iterative process.

Now that you've begun to home in on some key networks and identify what they can provide for themselves, it's time to start thinking about how your company fits in to the picture. For each of your top networks, answer the following questions with regard to the needs you believe they could self-serve.

WHAT DOES THE NETWORK NEED IN ORDER TO SELF-SERVE? A software platform is usually a part of the equation, but the needs may go further. Members of the network may need a way to prove their credentials and value to each other. Training and certification programs are useful in highly technical areas. A simple ratings system, such as those used by Airbnb, Uber, and Yelp, also can be useful in almost any network setup.

The network members might also benefit from other physical supplies or technical devices, such as the Nest thermostat or the Nike+ running monitor, to help them gather the data they need. Another point: you may want to conduct events and offer incentives to facilitate interaction among network participants.

HOW CAN YOUR COMPANY PARTNER WITH THE NETWORK? Next, identify whether your company has the assets and capabilities to fulfill network members' needs. If you don't, are there any potential partners you could reach out to for a solution? For example, Nike and Apple partnered to integrate Nike+ with the iPod.

WHAT WOULD YOU (LIKE TO) GET OUT OF THIS SCENARIO? There are many possibilities here. Remember that because operating a network requires the ability to make real-time changes in response to member demands, you may change your mind about what you now think you want from the network.

Of course, revenue is always an option. You could charge subscription fees for accessing the network, or transaction fees for using it. You could also sell advertising or access to outside parties. But direct revenue is only the beginning. Your organization could also generate a great deal of customer data that could be useful for outreach, product design, and more.

A network can also serve primarily to increase customer affinity—increasing brand awareness, supporting customer success, and creating avenues for customer feedback and co-creation.

Bringing Together the Network and the Organization

Now is the time to reflect and make a decision. You have thought carefully about your networks, the needs of the participants, and the networks' ability to self-serve. You have also considered the role your firm could play in facilitating this self-service, and the value that doing so could provide. How do you feel about the possibilities you've created? Does one network stand out among the rest?

You may need to iterate between the network value cycle and the company value cycle multiple times before you hit on a model that seems like a genuine opportunity.

We suggest that you select the network, and need, that you find most inspiring—whether the inspiration stems from the value to your firm

or the value to the network. If none of the possibilities is inspiring, return to the network value cycle and the firm value cycle, and try new networks, new assets, and new ways of generating value. This is a good time to bring in outside thinking. You can use a peer, a reverse mentor, or a total stranger as a collaborator and sounding board.

We know that sounds strange, but think about your own life for a moment. Hasn't a sentence overheard in a diner, or an advertising slogan, or a random television commercial startled you by leading you to an insight? Remember that you're putting on network eyes—and very likely, it's the first time you've done so. Inspiration comes from all sorts of places! You know the old saying, we're sure: minds are like parachutes—they work better when they're open.

When you've selected a network and need that your company could serve, you will be ready to move on to the next choice: the digital platform.

Choosing the Platform

The platform is the place where your network participants come to interact and share value with each other and with your company. Because you want to take advantage of the rapid scaling potential of technology, the platform must be digital. Your platform could take various forms, depending on the type of value that the network members are sharing: if they're selling goods or services, the platform needs to be a marketplace; if they're sharing information, it needs to be a good forum for communication; if they're generating data, you may need to develop a physical device in addition to the software platform.

Detail the specifications for the platform as you would for any software development project. We recommend that you begin small because iteration will be required. There are many off-the-shelf solutions (for example, online forums and e-commerce platforms) that will suffice for the first year or more of a new network initiative. Determine which digital technologies—social, mobile, cloud, big data analytics, and the internet of things—will be important for success.

With your specifications written, think critically about the current talents and capabilities within your organization. Review your physical, human, and intellectual capital inventories. If this network initiative is a departure from your normal state of business, you likely do not have the talent or technological assets you need to develop or manage the platform. In the next step, Operate, you will tackle these missing pieces. For now, focus on the ideal platform, even if you're certain you don't have the talent to create it.

Making It Real

You're picking up steam, but you've probably noticed that we haven't yet covered all the elements in the business model diagram. Although you have planned the foundation—who the key players are, what they will contribute, what they will receive, and how they will interact—there is still the crucial task of implementing your new vision. You will need to build, staff, and manage it. You will tackle these pieces in the next chapter.

The Enterprise Visualize Story

The Enterprise leadership team members were taken aback by how hard it was to complete the inventory process when they realized how little they knew about the resident and partner communities they served. But Terri Ludwig's vision was clear: the mission was to help people move up and out of poverty. Building housing was only a means to an end, and not an end in itself.

During its Visualize journey, the Enterprise team realized that a network focused on underserved end users—low-income families—was inspiring, but it was far beyond Enterprise's current competencies. The leaders realized that they would have more success beginning with their business relationships, which were much stronger and better understood. Therefore, they proposed an initial investment in a B2B network connecting their suppliers and partners, eventually transitioning into

a B2C network with end users. After the board approved the capital to fund this plan, the leaders were off to the races.

CIO Pradip Sitaram identified the need to build additional apps to serve three audiences: internal Enterprise workers; the partner community; and, in the long run, the resident community. He also needed to understand more about each group's needs so that he could build the apps on a standard platform in order to follow standard technology best practices: build it once and use it many times.

Enterprise also needed to begin restructuring the organization around its new theory of value—to use digitally enabled network orchestration to support low- and moderate-income families. The executives knew that they could expand the digital platform that Sitaram had already created for Enterprise's internal team, but it was a big undertaking to turn it outward to serve the B2B community and eventually the residents.

Reshaping the organization was not going to be an easy task, and everyone knew it. But they also knew that accessing and serving the B2B network would create a differentiated level of value and a new organizational design. In addition, the team members knew that low- and moderate-income families still had high levels of access to mobile phones and that the organization's network offering would allow Enterprise to reach and serve the needs of a broader population. Through the resident- and partner-centered apps, Enterprise would seek to organize and orchestrate relationships with the large health care, transportation, educational, and finance providers their residents and developers needed, as well as help the community members support each other. To do that, Enterprise needed to bring its twenty-five hundred partners into a large-scale digital ecosystem.

The new vision presented by Ludwig and Enterprise president Charlie Werhane was inspiring: to create a ten times or hundred times impact by restructuring the company to create "one Enterprise, one operating system, and one technology"—an arrangement that let the organization go beyond its traditional asset focus to serve end users (residents).

Some board members went so far as to say that this approach was "the greatest vision that had been presented since the firm's inception by Jim Rouse," the famous developer of Baltimore Harbor, New York's South Street Seaport, and Boston's Faneuil Hall.

This network vision was presented to the board and approved in September 2015. The hard work of operationalizing the vision—to transform Enterprise from an asset financier and service provider to a digitally enabled network orchestrator—was still ahead.

OPERATE

Enact Your Network Business Model

When you innovate, you've got to be prepared
for people to tell you that you are nuts.

—Larry Ellison, former CEO, Oracle

WHAT DOES IT TAKE FOR A LARGE FIRM TO INNOVATE? LET'S look at Google, one of the most innovative companies of the past decade, and its secret lab, X, previously known as Google X. Google is well known for its capability with digital technology and for its ability to innovate, and it has developed a specific structure and process for nurturing its most innovative projects, the ones it calls "moonshots."

In 2010, Google created X to develop a self-driving car. Since then, new projects have been added, such as Google Glass, a wearable computer with an optical head-mounted display; and Project Loon, which aims to bring the internet to everyone via a network of high-altitude balloons. Although Google is a company of many talents, some of these

moonshots fall well outside its standard competencies, just as network orchestration does for most organizations.

Because Google has had to figure out how to best manage and operate these projects, it can provide a great perspective for other companies looking to innovate their business models. Here are some of Google's best practices for managing innovative projects within a large company.

- *Separation.* X's labs are located in a physically separate space, about a half-mile from Google's main campus, and have a different reporting structure. This helps insulate Google Xers from the bureaucracy and potential meddling of the broader corporation.
- *Low investment.* Google invests judiciously in its moonshots. Former spokeswoman Jill Hazelbaker notes, "The sums involved are very small by comparison to the investments we make in our core businesses."[1]
- *The right talent.* X projects benefit from passionate leaders having relevant experience. For example, when embarking on the self-driving car project, the team brought on Sebastian Thrun, who previously sent an autonomous car through a seven-mile obstacle course in the Mojave Desert.
- *The external network.* Google leverages external experts to support its projects. It has partnered with at least sixteen other companies so far, ranging from Silicon Valley start-ups to established chip manufacturers.

All these criteria—separation, low investment, the right talent, and the external network—make for an open space in which teams can be innovative and almost instantly responsive to market feedback. All are necessary for creating a new, networked business within asset builder, service provider, and technology creator companies.

PIVOT Step 4: Operate

The goal of the Operate step is to get your new network business up and running with the components and processes that will help your company, and the network, achieve success.

During this step, you will address the funding, talent, and technology needs of your new network business, and you will create strategies for successfully managing the business within your broader organization and for managing the external network.

Beginning to Operate Your Network

This step is where the rubber meets the road. You and your team will begin to make your network vision a reality.

Many components need to be in place for your network business to start operating independently and generating results. In the Operate step, you move down one level in the business model framework and get practical about what you need to manage your network business internally (including the platform and team) and externally (focused on the network).

To begin, you need to make a crucial decision: selecting the person to lead and manage your network initiative. We will refer to this key person as the *network leader*, and he has a big job ahead of him. A successful network leader must be trusted by the leadership team, because he needs the freedom to make decisions independently and rapidly. The network leader also needs to be excited by the opportunity to cultivate a network business and should know the target network intimately.

The network leader should lead the decision-making process during this step. Although the executive team and board will have the final decision on the allocation of capital to technology and talent as well as the management structure for the team, it is the network leader's job to do the thinking up front, guided by this chapter, and make recommendations for setting up the new business for success.

Once the network leader is chosen and starts designing an operating plan, your organization can start to fill in the rest of the team, create the platform, and get your network functioning. Although operating is an ongoing activity, it usually takes two to four months to get the network business model up and running.

Because the platform sits at the heart of the network organization, we begin there. You have visualized a platform to enable your network members to serve their own needs. Now you will identify what it will take for your company to realize that platform.

Creating Your Platform

Three basic things are required to get your network platform operational: the technology to enable network interactions, the talent to create that technology and manage the network, and the capital to support the first two.

For technology, begin by reviewing the specifications that you created in the Visualize step. What technology assets do you need? Consider both physical technology, such as devices and servers, and intangible technology, such as software, websites, and apps. All digital network businesses will require intangible technology, but a few may need physical technology as well.

Then determine which of these technology assets you already have, and which will need to be sourced internally or externally. Refer to the complete inventory you created earlier. We'd like to give you more context on creating the platform, but the truth is that the platform can take so many different forms that we can't guess whether an off-the-shelf solution will work for you, whether you will need a custom solution, which specific technologies you will need to use, and so on.

Part of your success with a digital platform will depend on having the right talent—if not to build it, then at least to manage it. Consider the skills that will be essential to create and manage the technology and the network. In addition to building the platform, you will need team members who are skilled at evangelizing the network, incentivizing

participation, and co-creating with the network members. Finding passionate talent, with the right skill sets, to support the project is key to success. You probably do not want people doing this part-time on top of another role that already fully utilizes them.

Consider what roles your network team will need; developers, marketers, and domain experts are certainly in order. Then identify the characteristics and skills each role will require. Refer to your human capital breakdown to determine whether you currently have the talent to fill these roles.

Finally, assess the capital needs. Very likely, there is a gap between your current assets and what you need to operate your network business. Filling this gap will require capital, and there are several ways to manage costs.

When it comes to technology, you may find that an off-the-shelf platform will serve your needs, at least for the short term. Network outreach can even begin on free platforms such as Twitter, Facebook, or LinkedIn. Network orchestration businesses usually require significant iteration and input from the network in order to reach a mutually beneficial state, so be conservative with your early investments. Try a few things and get feedback before you make a major investment in new technology and talent.

Another option for reducing costs is to find a partner. When Nike decided to launch its sports ecosystem, Nike+, it partnered with Apple to help share the burden of design, testing, and marketing. Consider whether partnership is a good option for your firm; partners often can bring both talent and technology, and they can help reduce risk.

Once you've identified your technology, talent, and capital gaps, you can start creating a plan to fill them. In each case, this will require careful consideration of your capabilities, relationships, and time line. Technology can be developed in-house, but for most legacy firms, a faster and more reliable option is to purchase or partner.

When it comes to talent, if you don't have it in-house, you can use contractors, or even service firms, to fill the gap. But remember this

key point: if you believe, as we do, that digital technology is becoming required for market success, and that network orchestration is the most valuable business model, then you will eventually want to have this talent in-house. So factor in its acquisition to your long-term plan.

The last gap to close is the money itself. Creating plans for technology and talent will help you figure out how much you need. For most organizations this requires a commitment to diverting a part of investment capital to the creation of network businesses. You probably already have investment capital that is spent on new business generation and growth. Now that you know that network orchestration is the most scalable, profitable, and rapidly growing business model, it seems obvious that you should ensure that part of this allocation goes to network businesses.

Managing the Network Business In-House

With a plan for platform development, talent, and funding in place, it's time to think about how to manage the network initiative within your existing organization. Our experience has made it clear that innovation within a larger firm is extremely difficult. Here are a few factors that often derail the best-laid innovations.

- *Internal politics.* Wrangling between division leaders and jealousy over funding and prestige can divert attention and money away from the development of the network asset.
- *Lack of focus.* New projects can wither on the vine when employees must split their time between old responsibilities (with clear expectations) and new projects (with less clarity).
- *Undifferentiated performance targets.* New initiatives struggle to match the performance of existing business units, often for the first several years. Yes, years. New projects held to the standards of tried-and-true business units may be deemed failures before they have a chance to blossom.

- *Lack of patience.* Network organizations in particular require multiple iterations before they strike the right chord with their network members and begin generating revenue. An inexperienced network innovator may see these as failures, rather than progress. Thomas Edison found ten thousand ways not to invent the light bulb before he found the one right one.

- *Misaligned reporting structure.* Innovative initiatives must exist somewhere within the company, and often they get rolled into another division. The division leader may mismanage the initiative, because it doesn't fit the broader mission.

With these risks, it's important to think critically about how to create a structure to manage, support, and measure the network business model appropriately and with reasonable expectations.

While your network business is in the early stages of growth, it requires a different style of management from the rest of the firm. You need to make several strategic decisions about the management of this fledgling business. Here are our recommendations.

- *Reporting structure.* The team should report to a chain of command in which each manager understands, buys into, and supports the vision. This may require that the team report to an unusually senior person to begin, and this is fine. While the network business is going through early iterations and rapid development, it shouldn't be managed with close oversight anyway.

- *Decision authority.* The team needs to iterate rapidly and should be given authority to act independently, without an approval process, to the broadest degree possible. When approval is required, it should be an expedited process compared with that of the rest of the firm.

- *Focus.* The best practice is for team members to be focused only on the network initiative so that their attention is not divided.

This prevents politicking over time allocation, and it's helpful for team cohesion.

- *Expectations.* Expectations for this different, and brand-new, business model cannot be the same as for other, established business units. There should be performance targets for the network initiative, but leaders need to recognize that the path will be slow and convoluted at first.
- *Communication.* Innovation always runs the risk of creating concern or resentment within the rest of the organization. Network initiatives are naturally public, so leaders should manage internal sentiment by ongoing communication of the project's goals and alignment with the broad company mission.

Creating a new management style specific to the network business is key to growing it from a tiny seed into a new core business.

Managing the Network

The last step in operating your network is to create a plan for network management. Success at network orchestration requires a happy, invested, rewarded, and fast-growing network. The network, and its happiness, creates the value in network orchestration, so spend some time planning how to keep your network happy and engaged.

You need to decide how you will reward the members for their participation. Will they receive shared revenue, as do Uber drivers and Airbnb hosts? Esteem, like LinkedIn article contributors? Information, like Yelp or TripAdvisor participants? There are many possibilities, and your loyalty and growth programs must be tailored to the type of value the participants will receive.

You should also think about how you will maintain the loyalty of your network. Decide what types of communications and interactions will be beneficial between the network and your organization, and also among the participants. Create a plan to encourage high levels of activity.

Finally, think about how the network will grow. Networks are often self-reinforcing, because a larger network increases the potential value for each participant. However, most network companies also actively encourage growth through referral fees and other perks. Determine for your own network how you will attract new members.

The new-member question is particularly important in the beginning. You will need a plan for network start-up: how will you attract network members to participate when your platform is just getting up and running?

There are several possibilities. One is to seed the network with content, products, or services generated by your company. This approach will help fill in the gaps until the network creates the content itself. Another option is to create added incentives for early adopters. Perhaps you could increase the revenue share for this group or provide other incentives.

If you care for your network, it will care for you, too. And, as you have seen, the reverse is also true.

What's Next?

Now that you've planned for the platform, the internal management, and the external management of your network business, your model is complete and ready to implement—and iterate and iterate.

How will you know how to iterate and what success looks like? You do it by measuring what matters in the network world. We discuss measurement more thoroughly in the next chapter.

The Enterprise Operate Story

With its new vision for the firm approved by the board, the Enterprise team was ready to begin reallocating its capital and creating its new digital network platforms. CIO Pradip Sitaram, who had been deeply involved in evangelizing and envisioning Enterprise's transformation, took on the leadership role to move the network business from a vision to a reality.

Sitaram had already helped Enterprise create an internal network, based on Salesforce.com (a well-established cloud provider), which was used by employees and team members to chat, collaborate, originate loans, manage financial assets, and perform a multitude of business operations. This project was nearing completion, but Enterprise still had a team of about thirty internal technologists, and access to thirty-five others through a relationship with an offshore technology firm.

The Enterprise leadership team felt that this group, under Sitaram's leadership, had the skills needed to expand the internal network so that it could also serve the network of twenty-five hundred suppliers and partners, including developers, investors, and public policy experts. After careful planning, the board approved an additional capital investment in a digital network for partners and suppliers, as well as $1.8 million to begin development of the resident network, subject to final budget submission.

Sitaram was excited to turn this network, previously viewed as nothing more than a business operations support system, into co-creators to fulfill the Enterprise mission. He built out his team with three product managers—one to manage the internal network, one for the external business and partners network, and the third for the resident network. With funding pending approval, and an inspiring vision, the team got to work.

TRACK

Measure What Matters for a Network Business

Information is the oil of the 21st century, and analytics is the combustion engine.

—Peter Sondergaard, senior vice president, Gartner Research

AMAZON.COM HAS WHAT JEFF BEZOS CALLS A "CULTURE OF metrics." Amazon tracks its performance against about five hundred measurable goals, nearly 80 percent of them related to customer objectives. It gathers so much data about customers that it eschews classic customer segments—"millennial outdoorsman," "preteen fashionista"—in favor of segments of one: you.

When a visitor comes to Amazon.com, she's greeted with a home page covered in personal recommendations tailored to her and based on her browsing history, purchase history, and Amazon's best guesses of what will interest her based on comparison to the thousands of other shopper profiles. In fact, Amazon is getting so good at knowing its customers, at predicting what they want, that in 2014 it filed a patent for "anticipatory

shipping." Amazon believes that it will someday be able to predict what its customers want so accurately that it will begin the shipping process before the orders are even placed.

If you haven't heard, this deep data strategy is paying off. Amazon has one of the best customer satisfaction ratings in the United States, and it translates that wealth of customer data into new customer-satisfying innovations like the Kindle, Amazon streaming, and Amazon Web Services.

Maintaining specific, measurable goals and tracking key metrics, leaders at Amazon can make decisions quickly and confidently, with the best information possible. The rapid iteration required of digital innovation—particularly for network businesses—requires this type of support.

PIVOT Step 5: Track

The goal of Track, an ongoing process, is to determine which metrics and which reporting frequency you need to best support the development of your network business. You will create metrics to track the health of the three key components: the network, the platform, and the internal team. Additionally, you will determine the cadence and timeliness required for this data. Finally, you will begin to think about experimentation.

Beginning to Track Your Network

Let's start by reviewing the network orchestration business model diagram. The key elements of network orchestration are the network, the company, and the platform where they interact. You should carefully measure and track each of these components. This information lets you judge the health and progress of your endeavor and lets you design experiments that will help you adapt and grow.

For the network and platform metrics, the network leader and her team should create a proposal, based on what team members think will be most important to gauging success in the network initiative, and share it with the organization's executive team members, who will

have final approval. Because of their closeness to the project, network team members will also create the structure, whether organizational or technical, to gather the data to report on these metrics. For example, to track the number of network participants and the number of interactions, you will need a reporting dashboard within the platform itself.

For the internal team metrics, the supervising executive team will need to determine which metrics are most important for judging the success of the network team, and it usually makes sense for the network leader to gather the data and regularly report upward.

With the responsibilities laid out, let's discuss what most network organizations need to report on.

Tracking the Network

We start with the network, because your new business model revolves around a network focus. There are numerous items that can be measured, but a few themes are mandatory, such as size, growth, activity, and sentiment. How exactly you measure each of these dimensions depends on the specifics of your network business, but here we offer a few suggestions:

- *Size of the network.* Usually this is the number of human beings active in your network, but it could be households or families; for transacting networks, it could also be the number of products or services for sale. For example, Airbnb also tracks the number of properties available, and eBay tracks the number of listings.
- *Level of network activity.* You can measure network activity by tracking the number of transactions, interactions, postings, or communications generated by the participants.
- *Value created by the network.* For transactional networks, this is often measured by the amount of money or value of the goods exchanged. For networks where the value is esteem- or relationship-based, the value might be the number of new connections, the number of positive reviews, or the number of likes.

- *Network sentiment.* A happy network is loyal, productive, and likely to advocate. To track sentiment, you can watch service requests or other complaints, and you can regularly reach out to the network members for direct feedback. You can also track what is said about your network on social media sites such as Twitter and Facebook.
- *Network loyalty.* You can gauge loyalty by monitoring the number of repeat transactors or participants, and, for networks that require an active subscription, by watching the attrition rate.
- *Network growth rate.* This measures how quickly the number of participants is growing. You should also look for trend lines in all the other key metrics.

For each dimension, write down the specific metrics that you believe will help you assess the health of your network. There may also be key metrics unique to your endeavor, so consider whether additional metrics will be important, and add them to your list.

Frequency and timeliness are also important. Recall that one of the key differentiators of big data is the speed of gathering and the relevance of the data. For each metric on your list, note the cadence at which the metric should be tracked—hourly, daily, weekly, monthly, or quarterly—and the lag time that would be acceptable. For example, do you need real-time data, or is it acceptable to review a week's data one week later? Be realistic about these answers. Most leadership teams can track and respond to only the most essential numbers on an everyday, real-time basis.

Finally, create a goal for each metric that you hope to achieve within the first six months of your network's operation.

Tracking the Platform

The platform is what enables the network to do its thing—serve itself and interact with your company—and it needs to be in top shape.

Several items are always important for understanding platform health. How exactly you measure each of these dimensions depends on the specifics of your network business.

- *Ease of use.* To assess usability, you can track requests for help and support as well as incomplete transactions, and also poll the network directly.
- *Uptime versus downtime.* This is easy to track, but important. If your platform is down, it will frustrate the members and halt value creation.
- *Number of interactions.* To track platform interactions, look at the number of log-ons and transactions that take place on the platform on a daily, weekly, and monthly basis.
- *Number of active users.* This is simply the number of network participants who have active profiles on your platform at any time. You will need to define what "active" means to you; it could be anything from "created a profile last year" to "used the platform within the past week."

For each dimension, note the specific metrics that will help your organization judge the health of your platform, and add any other metrics that we have missed that are specific to your business.

Just as you did for network metrics, determine the cadence at which the metric should be tracked—hourly, daily, weekly, monthly, or quarterly—and the acceptable time lag. Then create a goal for each metric that you hope to achieve within the first six months of operation.

Tracking the Team

In truth, if your network and platform metrics look good, you probably don't need to worry too much about your team. They are doing their jobs. However, we have found that it's important to specifically think about the health of your internal team, particularly because often it is

working in a very different culture and using a different mental model from the rest of the organization.

Here are a few items that are useful, but again you need to tailor the specific metrics to your organization, business, and team.

- *Team morale.* Network initiative teams can become isolated from the broader company and also may face frustrating expectations and growth hurdles. It's important to keep your team members happy and focused so that they can be productive.
- *On-time and on-budget projects.* Because this is a new area for your organization, sometimes budget and time predictions can be significantly off. Be sure to track this closely so that expectations can be realigned when necessary.
- *Direct interactions with the network.* Creating intimacy with the network will require the active participation of the team. Team members have no chance of understanding and serving the network if they're always focused on implementing new features or running experiments. Make sure that each team member spends time *in* the network and interacting with participants each week.

Some of these goals and metrics are harder to track than others, because they don't happen online or on your platform. Think carefully about how you will track the health of your internal team as they work to grow your network business. You may need to attend team meetings every week or have regular one-on-ones with team members. Determine the cadence at which you will assess the health of your team, and create goals for each of the metrics.

Experimenting and Adapting

Once you're able to measure and track the status of your network, platform, and internal team, you can take specific steps to improve the key measures. After all, the purpose of measurement isn't only knowing but also planning strategic actions based on that knowledge.

Ongoing experimentation must be part of the internal team's mandate in order to home in on the best ways to interact with and serve the network. And the team must have the autonomy to design, implement, and act on these experiments. Amazon and Google, for example, are known for their ongoing experimentation with new formats, incentives, algorithms, pricing, and more as ways to maximize value creation for themselves and the network. Your team will do the same thing but on a smaller scale, at least to start. Having a dashboard with all the key metrics in place will set the stage for clear and productive experimentation.

Brainstorm with your team on experiments that will help you determine how best to grow and evolve your network business. The experimental possibilities are endless, but be sure to consider factors such as marketing communications (both frequency and content), pricing mo dels, referral bonuses, and the designs of your website and apps.

The Enterprise Tracking Story

Tracking was the hardest part for the Enterprise team members; they simply didn't have the technology in place to gather and review this type of data, particularly because their digital communities were still under development. Even their tracking of physical assets was fairly low-tech. Although the human resources and enterprise resource planning systems were digitized, they weren't in the cloud and were only partially integrated with the other systems that Pradip Sitaram had built.

In fact, as of this writing, Enterprise is still developing its nonfinancial mission-centric metrics and reporting, which will be used to guide capital allocation across the organization. Sitaram's team made thoughtful recommendations about what should be tracked for each of the three networks (internal, suppliers/partners, and residents), and the technology team was working on a comprehensive road map that he had submitted to Terri Ludwig for her review.

The internal and B2B team members began quickly working on road maps and integration plans so that they could tie in to existing systems

and provide real-time dashboards that the management team and the board could use to steer the organization. At the same time, the resident (B2C) team began experimenting, on a small scale, by developing use cases and storyboards and reaching out to interview residents in some of the key communities.

Charlie Werhane knew that it was possible to gather network participants from the forty million families Enterprise could serve, but potential members needed a clear value proposition. Getting there required not only the firm's new vision—"one enterprise, one technology, and one operating system" (referring to culture)—but also good data to measure its progress and performance on this new journey.

Sitaram is eager to bring his technology to the market and help implement the vision that Ludwig has put forward. The whole team is eager to expand Enterprise's reach and serve ten times, or maybe even one hundred times, as many low- and moderate-income families as it does now. The goal, as always, is to help Enterprise achieve Jim Rouse's original vision when he said, "What can be, ought to be . . . with the will to make it so."

We will all have to wait and see.

REFLECTING ON PIVOT

CONGRATULATIONS. YOU HAVE MADE IT TO THE END OF THE PIVOT journey and are now ready to sit back and bask in the glow of your 8× multiplier and adoring network—you know, the one that's creating all kinds of value for your firm.

Or maybe not quite yet.

More likely, you're nurturing a fledgling network that will require a lot of care, attention, experimentation, and iteration to grow into a healthy business unit. And when it does, it may still be only a small portion of your business. Although significant network investment should nudge your multiplier, you won't see dramatic results until the core of your business itself has transformed to network orchestration.

But let's not discount the hard thinking and hard work that your organization has done on this journey, with each piece contributing to a clearer vision of the present and future. In the Pinpoint step, we hope you took a stark look at yourself and your organization, asked the honest questions, and judged fairly the kind of business model and mental model your organization uses, and why. When you did the Inventory step, you took the time to carefully sort out all your firm's assets, even those you didn't think were assets the week before.

To Visualize your network, you started thinking about the future, shaping a new business model in which value can be co-created and shared between your organization and a network. The Operate step helped you create a plan to realize this vision, and the Track step guided you in creating the metrics and experiments to shape and grow it.

We know from experience in working with leaders and boards that this work is difficult and exhausting. Consciously shifting one's mental model requires levels of openness and perseverance that most people struggle to attain. You may not have done this work perfectly, but that is a part of the process. It's a process—just like growing a network—that's endless.

We encourage you to keep at it. Grow the business you have started, learn, and repeat in other parts of the business, with other networks. Creating the second network goes faster than creating the first one; the third, faster still, as you become more adept at the PIVOT process.

Great value is available in the network, and if your organization doesn't access it, someone else will.

THE PRACTICE

PART FOUR

Becoming a Network Leader

LEADERS NEED TO THINK AND ACT DIFFERENTLY

If you never change your mind, why have one?

—Edward de Bono, physician, psychologist, and author of *Six Thinking Hats*

NEW BUSINESS MODELS REQUIRE NEW THINKING; SO LET'S START with three simple questions:

1. What beliefs and actions make a great business leader?
2. Do you believe that the answer changes over time?
3. How much have you changed your beliefs and actions over your career?

Obviously, thought leaders throughout the ages have promulgated different beliefs about value, leadership, technologies, and organizational design. Furthermore, different situations call for different strengths. But what is critical for a leader now? We assert that the beliefs and skills that

lead to success have changed dramatically in recent years and the most successful leaders will be those who can embrace new mental models.

Thirty years ago, when essentially all assets were tangible, the best corporate leaders were those who could acquire and finance assets, manage a tight manufacturing process, hire and manage thousands of people, operate well, and grow their businesses to a competitive scale. In 1985, lean manufacturing and Six Sigma were the buzzwords, and *Fortune's* most admired corporations were IBM, Coca-Cola, Dow Jones, 3M, and Hewlett-Packard.

A lot has changed in thirty years, but two changes stand out clearly: the growth and ubiquity of digital technology, and the ongoing rapid, and exponentially increasing, pace and magnitude of change. In 2015, *Fortune's* most admired companies were Apple, Google, Berkshire Hathaway, Amazon.com, and Starbucks, and a growing percentage of the *Forbes* wealthiest individuals are technologists or network leaders.

Apple, Google, Amazon.com, and Starbucks have made significant investments in digital technologies (if you're unsure about Starbucks, consider its popular app and payment system). What's more, they have responded with agility to market changes by changing their core beliefs about value and firm design.

- Apple, despite its reputation for maintaining tight control of its product line, opened its platform and created the Apple Developer Program, allowing anyone to develop apps for its products.

- Google, ever inventive, used Google Labs, and later X, as incubators for new ideas. Google expanded far beyond its search engine core into e-mail, social networking, enterprise software, high-speed internet, the Android operating system, and now self-driving cars and beyond.

- Amazon.com began as a book retailer but has steadily spiraled outward into consumer electronics, cloud computing services, and media development.

- Starbucks still innovates within its core—caffeinated beverages—but isn't afraid to tackle digital technology. Chief Digital Officer Adam Brotman began with the popular Starbucks app and expanded it into a payment system; in Q4 2014, 16 percent of US Starbucks transactions took place via mobile device.

What can we infer about the leaders of these admired companies? At a minimum, these companies are led by adaptive thinkers who are open to expanding their firms into uncharted territory and new business models. We've found that a great leader is willing to, and can (two different processes), shift his or her mental model to operate in a new way, in a new type of business, when, and as often as, the world changes.

Changing Your Beliefs Is Hard

Thinking about things differently is surprisingly difficult. And it's even harder for people whose thinking and habits to date have created great success—leaders like you. The average CEO has thirty years of business experience on which she habitually relies (and for board members, it is even higher). The neural pathways created in her brain by those years of experience run deep and feel reliable. But the world is a very different place now than it was even ten years ago. The same thinking, and the actions it drove, that led to market success in 2005, 1995, and 1985 are not likely to work now.

Ask yourself this: how long has it been since you have examined your core beliefs and the related actions? We don't mean your next vacation or what car to buy, but something that you truly care about—perhaps a closely held belief about life, family, or business. For most of us, this happens rarely, especially in business where industry best practices rule the day. David McRaney wrote as follows in his 2011 best seller, *You Are Not So Smart*.

> Once something is added to your collection of beliefs, you protect it from harm. You do this instinctively and unconsciously when

> confronted with attitude-inconsistent information. Just as confirmation bias shields you when you actively seek information, the backfire effect defends you when the information seeks you, when it blindsides you. Coming or going, you stick to your beliefs instead of questioning them.[1]

Although thinking differently is hard, and acting differently is even harder, it's imperative if you are serious about making the shift to become a network orchestrator.

Thinking Creates Action, and Action Creates Outcomes

Our thinking creates our actions—even if we're not conscious of our thoughts. This relationship is obvious to most people, because we understand generally that something must be happening in our brains in order to move our mouths and our feet. But try turning the statement around: all of our actions result from our thoughts and beliefs. This perspective brings a different nuance, because often we don't take time to reflect on the thoughts that motivate our habitual actions.

The term *mental model* refers to your internal beliefs, preferences, and biases—conscious or unconscious—about the world and the way it operates. There are some types of preferences that, after they're formed, we rarely reexamine. Much of our thinking becomes habitual and unexamined, resulting in habitual and rote action. Habit isn't necessarily a bad thing; leaving your toothbrush in the same place every night so that you can find it every morning is a good idea. But some habits get in the way of progress. Have yours?

Your *core beliefs* are deeply held beliefs about the way the world works. In business, core beliefs are often about what creates value and risk in industries and organizations. Core beliefs are so innate that we often perceive them as facts.

Our core beliefs lead us to create our *guiding principles*—the rules and ideals that we live by. These principles then drive how we allocate

The evolution of mental models

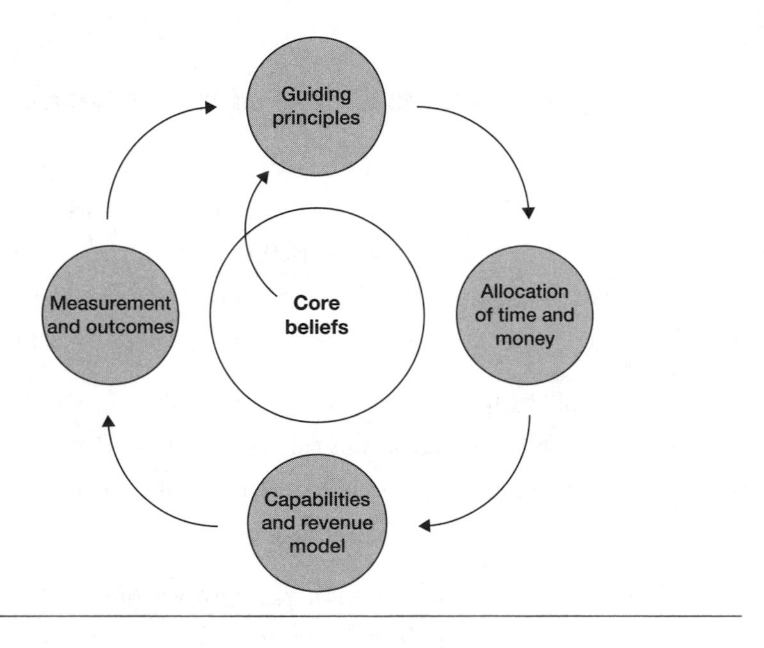

our time and money, what capabilities we develop and how we generate revenue, and ultimately how we measure success. Out of this cycle emerges our business model. You'll notice that at no point does an arrow point *back* into the core beliefs. That is because once we form them, we protect our core beliefs against counterpoints and arguments. The whole system surrounds, protects, and ultimately reinforces our core beliefs—and that makes it hard to change them.

Let's examine what this looks like with regard to business models. Most leaders of asset-building companies believe that owning and controlling physical assets is the path to creating value. Therefore, they spend their money buying physical assets, and their time operating and managing them. The leader develops capability, and comfort, with these assets and the business model. He measures his success at managing physical goods, adjusts his guiding principles slightly, and the cycle continues. At no point does the leader seriously reconsider whether physical assets create the best path to value, and whether those assets need to be

designed, created, and maintained using internal resources. Instead, he focuses on being a better asset builder.

Network Leaders Have Different Beliefs

As you would expect, network orchestrators take a perspective that's different from the one taken by legacy leaders. Network orchestrators invest in different assets, create different relationships, and manage people differently because they have taken on a different way of thinking about the world—a different mental model. Here are examples:

- Traditional thinking holds that companies need to be large-scale to reduce unit costs and stay competitive. *Network thinkers leverage intangible assets and external networks to achieve very low marginal costs from the beginning.*
- Traditional thinking advises that employees must be carefully managed to maximize output. *Network thinkers believe that employees, or network partners, who manage their own work create more value.*
- Traditional thinking believes that financial accounting provides a thorough view of a company's health and viability. *Network thinkers believe that a complete view comes only when you add measures of intangible assets, such as customer loyalty and employee engagement.*

What makes network orchestration difficult to develop is that it is not just an adjustment or "tweak" of previous business models. In many cases, the network way of thinking directly contradicts previous management norms. Network orchestration is not merely the next model in a progression from asset builder, to service provider, to technology creator. In fact, the business models are not a progression at all. Instead, network orchestration takes leaders into uncharted territory, leveraging the great networks that lie outside traditional company boundaries, not

just the assets and employees within its control. This is why we recommend an approach to transformation with incremental change, guided by the PIVOT process.

Inverting Your Core Beliefs

If you want to become a leader who embraces the newest assets and technologies and capitalizes on them, then you need to start the never-ending process of examining and adapting your core beliefs. With our clients, we use a five-step process we've developed over the years for uncovering and adapting core beliefs. We call this process *inversion*: considering ideas that are the opposite of your habitual ones. Here are the steps:

1. **Identify** how your core beliefs manifest themselves in your business. Refer back to the figure on page 193 and document your guiding principles, time and capital allocation patterns, primary skills and capabilities, and the key metrics and outcomes that you track. For the leader of an asset building company, most of these dimensions would revolve around the efficient production and management of physical goods.
2. **Uncover** the core beliefs that motivate these behaviors and priorities. This step usually takes some ongoing reflection, and the result might be something you wouldn't want to admit to your peers. Industry best practices likely influence your thinking. Focus on your beliefs about assets, value creation, and business model. For example, a core belief could be, "Physical assets are durable and reliable; digital networks volatile and risky," or "The value that my employees provide for our customers is irreplaceable."
3. **Invert** the core belief and consider the implications. There are many possible inversions in each instance. For example, in response to the belief about physical assets above, one could

think, "Physical assets are actually riskier than other assets," or "Digital networks help firms reduce risk." Find an inversion that resonates with you—one that you think might actually be true—and consider how this new belief would change your guiding principles, asset allocation, capabilities, and key metrics.

4. **Extrapolate** what implications these new core beliefs and the resulting principles, asset allocation, capabilities, and metrics would have for your business. Observe what is happening in your industry and, more broadly, how different core beliefs might help you address or prevent disruption. Consider the implications these beliefs could have for your customers, employees, suppliers, and investors. For most leaders, new core beliefs often reveal previously unconsidered possibilities and options.
5. **Act** on the new core beliefs by sharing them with your leadership team and adapting your guiding principles, asset allocation, capabilities, and metrics. Consciously changing your actions, particularly with regard to capital allocation, is an important part of the process and helps reinforce the changes in thinking you are trying to achieve. Ultimately, these changes will alter your overall business model, bolstering your long-term success and survival.

At any point in the process, feel free to take a step back, revise, and iterate. Over time you will home in on the beliefs and practices that best suit you, your organization, and industry.

Most Innovators Are Inverting Old Beliefs

Most industry-changing innovations are based on new beliefs. Netflix is a prime example. From the outside, Reed Hastings, Netflix's CEO, observed that many of the video rental and movie industry's core beliefs and supporting systems (physical stores and movie theaters with transactional revenue models) were failing to make customers happy. He questioned each and every one of them, inverted them, and brought

them to market. On-demand home delivery of movies with no late fees was a revelation for the market; it constituted a major disruption. This new business model took down Blockbuster and has forced movie theaters to adapt and find new ways to lure customers off their sofas to the big screen.

Today this story is familiar and can be seen in many industries. Uber's CEO, Travis Kalanick, did the same thing when he created a ride-sharing service using mobile technologies to connect drivers and riders directly, where existing black car and taxi companies didn't. Founder of Angie's List Angie Hicks connected homeowners to share reviews of local businesses and service providers, creating enormous value over traditional listings like the Yellow Pages.

But don't assume that only start-ups can embrace new mental models and core beliefs. General Motors is demonstrating that it too can shift its core beliefs about value with a $500 million investment in the ride-sharing start-up Lyft and a commitment to build digital networks and autonomous vehicles.

Take It Outside Your Mind and into the Real World

As you update your mental model, you need to take reinforcing actions to help realize the change. Here's what we recommend.

TAKE IN NEW INFORMATION, NEW DATA, AND NEW IDEAS. As a leader in business, you probably already keep up with the latest news and the ways others are thinking, but, as we've said, all of us naturally have a bias toward perspectives like our own. In fact, we automatically select ideas that reinforce our own. You need to work to incorporate a more diverse perspective into your daily updates. Keep tabs on industries a bit further afield, particularly on trends in the advancement and use of technology.

Within your own organization, spend time with the groups that normally get less of your attention. Ask them about their priorities, concerns, and ideas for innovation.

WRITE NEW STORIES. You probably have an elevator pitch for yourself, and another for your company, that you pull out on autopilot when needed—a short story that cuts right to the heart of your strengths and purpose. For example, you might say you're a "seasoned operations expert who can quickly identify waste and motivate a team to fix it." You work for a "large-format, value-oriented grocery and general goods retailer." To change your thinking, don't let the stories you've told in the past limit your options for the future. Let the stories of the past stay in the past.

As you read this book and identify shifts and opportunities that make sense for your firm, start telling yourself and others new stories about what you are and what you're becoming. Be bold. You can always scale back, but without that big stretch, you'll tend to stay within your habits.

BREAK HABITS. Once you start to grasp the edges of your current mental model, you will start identifying times when it puts you on autopilot. These are times when you operate quickly or habitually in line with your old mental model without taking time to consider whether it's the right decision for this particular instance. The fastest way to break old habits is, paradoxically, to slow down.

For example, when you're allocating budget, deciding whom to invite to a meeting, or choosing whom to interview, you probably have some rules of thumb based on an outdated perspective of the world, yourself, or your company. You need to change your routine for making these decisions and try out a new mental model, if only a few times. For example, invite a representative of every division to a meeting that is usually more exclusive, or ask the people in your star business unit to justify their budget.

SEEK AN OUTSIDE PERSPECTIVE. Ask for counsel or mentorship from individuals who have different mental models from your own. Although they might exist within your company, it is far more likely that they're external—outside your industry, outside your demographics, outside your comfort zone.

Technological mentorship is especially important for anyone wanting to ride the digital network wave. CEO.com found in 2015 that 61 percent of CEOs have no social media presence whatsoever.[2] They're not on Twitter, Facebook, Instagram, or LinkedIn. Perhaps we can agree that they may not be tuned in to the nuances of millennials, 88 percent of whom use Facebook regularly to get news and information.[3]

Reverse mentorship—in which a younger employee provides the mentoring for someone more senior—is a great option for those who want to experience a new mental model or gain technological perspective. Reverse mentoring was popularized by GE CEO Jack Welch, who learned how to surf the internet from an employee in her twenties.

Gaining a new mental model seems a dangerous goal for someone who has been successful in her career. After all, almost all of us would agree on the truism, If it ain't broke, don't fix it. But many of our business habits aren't aging well—and a new generation of disruptors is right around the corner, and the next generation is right around the next one. To change your habits, you need to make the effort to try on new perspectives. Even if some of them don't fit, the experience will open your mind and will prove to be valuable.

Others Are at Work on Old Mental Models

In 2010, Jeff Immelt, CEO of General Electric, saw that GE needed to respond to the expansion of innovative digital technology into its primary sector: industrials. Rather than let new players consume the value that was created as his industry digitized, Immelt began to purposefully evolve the firm in the direction of digital networks.

Describing this transformation to McKinsey, Immelt said, "We want to treat analytics like it's as core to the company over the next twenty years as material science has been over the past fifty years. . . . We can evolve our business model accordingly."[4]

Immelt decided to develop the analytics capability in-house rather than through external acquisitions, but during the process he found

that norms and mental models throughout the organization needed to adapt. Describing the transformation that was required, Immelt conceded, "I thought if we hired a couple thousand technology people, if we upgraded our software, things like that, that was it. I was wrong. Product managers have to be different; salespeople have to be different; on-site support has to be different. We've had to drill and change a lot about the company. And I just think it's infecting everything we do . . . I think in a positive way."

What Immelt discovered is that business model transformation doesn't come about simply by changing a few outward behaviors. It requires a deeper change—leaders with new ideas that, in turn, create new behaviors throughout the organization.

Build a New Mental Model for the Network Age

When the environment is static, an old mental model is fine, or even good; you've had decades to polish it, after all. But when the environment is changing rapidly, an old mental model can prevent you from understanding the new environment, much less reacting to it effectively and benefiting from the new outcomes that new beliefs will deliver.

Are you willing to lead like Jeff Immelt in your organization and for your industry? Your willingness to change your mental model—through new stories, habits, perspectives, and ideas—will set the trend for other leaders in your firm. If you will challenge your historical viewpoint on each of the ten principles we raise in this book, and create a new digital network path for your firm, you will deliver unprecedented growth and value.

YOU ARE THE LEADER OF YOUR OWN NETWORK

A tree that shades a picnic begins as a mere sapling. A skyscraper begins as a hole in the ground. A journey of a thousand miles begins with one foot forward.

—Susan Corso, author, *Tao for Now*

TO REPEAT OUR REFRAIN, IT'S ALL ABOUT NETWORKS. THE WORLD has changed, and the sources and distribution of value are not the same as they were twenty years ago. These changes have unlocked the potential for enormous economic value, but, to get there, our organizations need to change.

We arrived at this spot because we started, many years ago, in a world without digital technology, without the internet, and without smartphones. During that time, we developed many best practices, operating procedures, and ideas about how businesses and organizations worked. We did the best we could with what we had. Now, with a lot more, we can do a better job of creating and capturing what is really, enduringly

valuable, be it things, labor, intellect, or relationships. We just need to adopt new, network-based mental and business models.

To get from here to there, all of us must accept that the way businesses have always been organized, led, and governed is not the only way. It's only "the way it's always been done." Now, remarkable digital advances and new network-based business models allow us to access the excess capacities and intangible assets that belong to each of us. Those organizations that create and orchestrate networks are benefiting from this core understanding, and will benefit well into tomorrow. And for good reason: the rewards are great.

Network orchestrators grow faster, create greater profits, scale at nearly zero cost, and earn the best multipliers from investors, who are already beginning to reallocate capital based on the business model. On top of that, the leaders, partners, and customers of network orchestrators benefit from fulfilling, mutually rewarding, and self-organizing relationships. To be a network business, organizations must do a lot of work. To achieve network value, leaders must pivot their people, processes, pricing, products, and entire mental models, entering into the network realm. When organizations spend less time making, selling, and owning, and spend more time inviting, accessing, and sharing, the outcome is different for everyone.

From the organization side, there is a new focus on accessing the initiative, ideas, creativity, and relationships of employees and customers (and this practice can extend even to investors, suppliers, distributors, and more).

From the consumer side, people enjoy increased openness and fulfillment of broader desires. Customers want to interact more deeply with their favorite brands—communicating on social media, sharing promotions, contributing to product development or advertising, and generally creating a mutual, symbiotic relationship that goes far beyond the normal money-for-products exchange.

From the investor side, less capital needs to be used, given that network organizations rely on the excess capacity of assets—including labor,

knowledge, and relationships—that already exist and have been developed. The result: more growth, at lower cost, with often greater returns.

Our final message is a personal one. The transformation of your firm into a network is dependent on a transformation of the people inside the firm—and, specifically, on you. Organizational change must begin with the action of a single motivated individual—someone like you.

Recognize that your different roles or personas—spouse, parent, leader, customer, investor, owner—are intertwined and interdependent. Bring your whole self to work, and back home, each day; that is how the rest of the world will view you anyway. And then bring that same attitude to your organization. The walls are coming down, and, like it or not, you are a member of the digital network. Given that, it is the responsibility of all of us to act with kindness, openness, and mutual respect. There is no other way.

It's time for all of our actions to reflect this reality: we are deeply intertwined with the networks that surround us, and we all have a lot to offer. Those leaders who reach out to the network with an open mind will find that they and their firms can give, and receive, more, based on the new open spaces that are created.

We wish you unprecedented success in this new world order we're co-creating and accessing. We have all the assets we need. We only need to access them.

May the power of the network be with us all. An abundant future awaits each and every one of us. It is our hope that this book will accelerate that reality.

For more information about creating network value, join the movement at openmatters.com.

NOTES

Digital Networks Are Eating the World

1. Nigel Fenwick with Peter Burris and Rachel Klehm, "Digital Predator or Digital Prey," Forrester Research, May 29, 2015, https://www.forrester.com/Digital+Predator+Or+Digital+Prey/fulltext/-/E-res120921.

Networks Have Big Advantages

1. Tatiana Serafin, "Exploring Strategic Risk," Deloitte Touche Tohmatsu Limited, 2013, http://www2.deloitte.com/content/dam/Deloitte/global/Documents/Governance-Risk-Compliance/dttl-grc-exploring-strategic-risk.pdf.
2. Nigel Fenwick and Martin Gill, "The Future of Business Is Digital," Forrester Research, 2014, http://blogs.forrester.com/f/b/users/NFENWICK/Infographic_1v4.pdf.
3. Joseph Bradley et al., "Digital Vortex: How Digital Disruption Is Redefining Industries," Global Center for Digital Business Transformation, 2015, http://www.imd.org/uupload/IMD.WebSite/DBT/Digital_Vortex_06182015.pdf.

Principle 1, Technology

1. Matthew Brunwasser, "A 21st-Century Migrant's Essentials: Food, Shelter, Smartphone," *New York Times*, August 25, 2015, http://mobile.nytimes.com/2015/08/26/world/europe/a-21st-century-migrants-checklist-water-shelter-smartphone.html?_r=0.
2. Yegge's comments have been reposted with permission on Google+, https://plus. google.com/+RipRowan/posts/eVeouesvaVX.
3. This and the following remarks are Simon Parkin, "What Zuckerberg Sees in Oculus Rift," *MIT Technology Review*, March 26, 2014, https://www.technologyreview.com/s/525881/what-zuckerberg-sees-in-oculus-rift/.
4. Julie Bort, "Cisco Chairman John Chambers Has an Idea for How the US Can Create Another 1 Million Jobs," Business Insider, September 30, 2015, http://www.businessinsider.com/cisco-chairman-john-chambers-has-idea-to-create-1-million-us-jobs-a-year-2015-9.

Principle 2, Assets

1. Ocean Tomo, press release, March 5, 2015, http://www.oceantomo.com/2015/03/04/2015-intangible-asset-market-value-study/.
2. "Study on Employee Engagement Finds 70% of Workers Don't Need Monetary Rewards to Feel Motivated," Badgeville, June 13, 2013, https://badgeville.com/study-

on-employee-engagement-finds-70-of-workers-dont-need-monetary-rewards-to-feel-motivated/.

3. Sara Horowitz and Fabio Rosati, "53 Million Americans Are Freelancing," Freelancers Union, September 4, 2014, https://www.freelancersunion.org/blog/dispatches/2014/09/04/53million/.

4. Jeff Wald, "5 Predictions for the Freelance Economy in 2015," *Forbes*, November 24, 2014, http://www.forbes.com/sites/waldleventhal/2014/11/24/5-predictions-for-the-freelance-economy-in-2015/.

Principle 3, Strategy

1. Bridget van Kralingen, "IBM's Transformation—From Survival to Success," *Forbes*, July 7, 2010, http://www.forbes.com/2010/07/07/ibm-transformation-lessons-leadership-managing-change.html.

2. Ibid.

3. Gregory Mankiw, *Principles of Economics* (Mason, OH: South-Western Cengage Learning, 2008).

4. Stephen Hall, "How to Put Your Money Where Your Strategy Is," *McKinsey Quarterly*, March 2012, http://www.mckinsey.com/insights/strategy/how_to_put_your_money_where_your_strategy_is.

5. Ibid.

Principle 4, Leadership

1. Stanley McChrystal et al., *Team of Teams: New Rules of Engagement for a Complex World* (New York: Portfolio/Penguin, 2015).

2. Ibid.

3. *The 2015 American Pantry Study*, Deloitte, June 2015, http://www2.deloitte.com/us/en/pages/consumer-business/articles/2015-american-pantry-study.html.

4. American Management Association website, http://www.amanet.org/news/10606.aspx.

5. Issie Lapowsky, "Ev Williams on Twitter's Early Years," *Inc.*, October 4, 2013, http://www.inc.com/issie-lapowsky/ev-williams-twitter-early-years.html.

6. "Walter Isaacson: Steve Jobs' Favorite Product Was the Team He Built at Apple," Big Think, 2015, http://bigthink.com/think-tank/steve-jobs-as-prickly-team-builder-with-walter-isaacson.

Principle 5, Customers

1. Lego Group website, "Mission and Vision," http://www.lego.com/en-us/aboutus/lego-group/mission-and-vision.

2. Andrew O'Connell, "Lego CEO Jørgen Vig Knudstorp on Leading through Survival and Growth," *Harvard Business Review*, January 2009, https://hbr.org/2009/01/lego-ceo-jorgen-vig-knudstorp-on-leading-through-survival-and-growth.

3. Brand Finance, press release, "Lego Overtakes Ferrari as the World's Most Powerful Brand," http://brandfinance.com/news/press-releases/lego-overtakes-ferrari-as-the-worlds-most-powerful-brand/.

4. Innocentive website, "What We Do," http://www.innocentive.com/about-innocentive.

Principle 6, Revenues

1. Brent Leary, "Amir Elaguizy of Cratejoy: Good Subscription Business Models Focus on Relationships Not Transactions," Small Business Trends, August 14, 2015, http://smallbiztrends.com/2015/08/elaguizy-cratejoy-subscription-business-models.html.

Principle 7, Employees

1. Travis Kalanick, "The Charms of the Sharing Economy," *Economist, The World in 2016* (single issue), November 6, 2015, http://www.theworldin.com/article/10631/charms-sharing-economy.

2. Ernst & Young, *Study: Work-Life Challenges across Generations*, http://www.ey.com/US/en/About-us/Our-people-and-culture/EY-work-life-challenges-across-generations-global-study.

3. Rena Rasch, "Your Best Workers May Not Be Your Employees," IBM Smarter Workforce Institute, October 2014, http://www-01.ibm.com/common/ssi/cgi-bin/ssialias?infotype=SA&subtype=WH&htmlfid=LOL14027USEN.

4. Adam Davidson, "What Hollywood Can Teach Us About the Future of Work," On Money, *New York Times,* May 5, 2015, http://www.nytimes.com/2015/05/10/magazine/what-hollywood-can-teach-us-about-the-future-of-work.html?_r=0.

5. Amy Adkins, "Majority of U.S. Employees Not Engaged Despite Gains in 2014," Gallup, January 28, 2015, http://www.gallup.com/poll/181289/majority-employees-not-engaged-despite-gains-2014.aspx.

6. Tammy Erickson, "The Rise of the New Contract Worker," HBR.org, September 7, 2012, https://hbr.org/2012/09/the-rise-of-the-new-contract-worker/.

7. Mike Myatt, "10 Reasons Your Top Talent Will Leave You," *Forbes*, December 13, 2012, http://www.forbes.com/sites/mikemyatt/2012/12/13/10-reasons-your-top-talent-will-leave-you/#39274873a149.

8. Mary Meeker, "Internet Trends 2015—Code Conference," KPCB, May 27, 2015, http://www.kpcb.com/internet-trends.

Principle 8, Measurement

1. Bernard Marr, "Big Data at Dickey's Barbecue Pit: How Analytics Drives Restaurant Performance," *Forbes*, June 2, 2015, http://www.forbes.com/sites/bernardmarr/2015/06/02/big-data-at-dickeys-barbecue-pit-how-analytics-drives-restaurant-performance/#34a989da3514.

2. Ibid.

3. Ocean Tomo, press release, "Ocean Tomo Releases 2015 Annual Study of Intangible Asset Market Value," March 5, 2015, http://www.oceantomo.com/blog/2015/03-05-ocean-tomo-2015-intangible-asset-market-value/.

4. Bradley Hope and Daniel Huang, "Firms Analyze Tweets to Gauge Stock Sentiment," *Wall Street Journal*, July 6, 2015, http://www.wsj.com/articles/tweets-give-birds-eye-view-of-stocks-1436128047.

5. Tom Davenport, "Three Big Benefits of Big Data Analytics," SAS, 2014, http://www.sas.com/en_us/news/sascom/2014q3/Big-data-davenport.html.

Principle 9, Boards

1. David Kesmodel and Annie Gasparro, "Inside Kellogg's Effort to Cash In on the Health-Food Craze," *Wall Street Journal*, August 31, 2015, http://www.wsj.com/articles/inside-kelloggs-effort-to-cash-in-on-the-health-food-craze-1441073082.

2. Spencer Stuart, "Spencer Stuart U.S. Board Index 2015," November 2015, https://www.spencerstuart.com/research-and-insight/spencer-stuart-us-board-index-2014.

3. Michael J. Silverstein and Kate Sayre, "The Female Economy," *Harvard Business Review*, September 2009, https://hbr.org/2009/09/the-female-economy.

4. Rick Newman, "Why U.S. Companies Aren't So American Anymore," *U.S. News and World Report*, June 30, 2011, http://money.usnews.com/money/blogs/flowchart/2011/06/30/why-us-companies-arent-so-american-anymore.

5. PwC, *Good to Grow: 2014 US CEO Survey*, 2014, http://www.pwc.com/us/en/ceo-survey-us/2014/assets/2014-us-ceo-survey.pdf.

6. Dorothy Enskog, "Women's Positive Impact on Corporate Performance," Credit Suisse, September 23, 2014, https://www.credit-suisse.com/us/en/news-and-expertise/research/credit-suisse-research-institute/news-and-videos.article.html/article/pwp/news-and-expertise/2014/09/en/womens-impact-on-corporate-performance-letting-the-data-speak.html.

7. Thomas Barta, Markus Kleiner, and Tilo Neumann, "Is There a Payoff from Top-Team Diversity?"*McKinsey Quarterly*, April 2012, http://www.mckinsey.com/insights/organization/is_there_a_payoff_from_top-team_diversity.

8. Rhys Grossman, Tuck Richards, and Nora Viskin, "2014 Digital Board Directory Study," Russell Reynolds Associates, January 29, 2015, http://www.russellreynolds.com/insights/thought-leadership/2014-digital-board-director-study.

9. David F. Larcker, Sarah M. Larcker, and Brian Tayan, *What Do Corporate Directors and Senior Managers Know about Social Media?* (New York: The Conference Board, 2012).

10. McKinsey & Company survey, "The Digital Tipping Point: McKinsey Global Survey Results," June 2014, http://www.mckinsey.com/insights/business_technology/the_digital_tipping_point_mckinsey_global_survey_results.

11. Estelle Metayer, "When Social Media Matters: A Guide to the Board of Directors for Better Governance," Competia, September 8, 2011, http://competia.com/when-social-media-matters-a-guide-to-the-board-of-directors-for-better-governance/.

12. Barta, Kleiner, and Neumann, "Is There a Payoff from Top-Team Diversity?"

13. Caroline Fairchild, "How Macy's Quietly Created One of America's Most Diverse Boards," *Fortune*, February 18, 2015, http://fortune.com/2015/02/18/macys-board-of-directors/.

14. L2, *Digital IQ Index: Department Stores 2014*, September 9, 2014, http://www.l2inc.com/research/department-stores-2014-2.

Principle 10, Mindset

1. Mike Isaac, "General Motors, Gazing at Future, Invests $500 Million in Lyft," *New York Times*, January 4, 2016.

2. Ibid.

3. Larry Page, Alphabet press release, August 11, 2015, https://abc.xyz/.

4. Brad Stone, *The Everything Store: Jeff Bezos and the Age of Amazon* (Boston, MA: Little, Brown and Company, 2013).

Introduction to PIVOT

1. Enterprise Community Partners website, "About Our Founders," http://www.enterprisecommunity.com/about/history/about-our-founders.

Pinpoint

1. Evan Bakker, "Bankers Across the Globe Expect Major Tech Companies to Cut Into Their Retail Banking Business," Business Insider, March 18, 2015, http://www.businessinsider.com/bankers-expect-their-retail-banking-revenue-to-fall-2015-3.
2. Barry Libert, Yoram (Jerry) Wind, and Megan Beck Fenley, "What Apple, Lending Club, and Airbnb Know about Collaborating with Customers," HBR.org, July 3, 2015, https://hbr.org/2015/07/what-apple-lending-club-and-airbnb-know-about-collaborating-with-customers; and "What Airbnb, Uber, and Alibaba Have in Common," HBR.org, November 20, 2014, https://hbr.org/2014/11/what-airbnb-uber-and-alibaba-have-in-common.
3. "Did You Know? Facts from Our Executive Compensation and Benefits (ECB) Proprietary Databases," Alvarez & Marsal, issue 8, November 10, 2014, http://www.alvarezandmarsal.com/sites/default/files/files/Age-CEO-CFO-COO.pdf.

Operate

1. Claire Cain Miller and Nick Bilton, "Google's Lab of Wildest Dreams," *New York Times*, November 13, 2011, http://www.nytimes.com/2011/11/14/technology/at-google-x-a-top-secret-lab-dreaming-up-the-future.html?_r=0.

Leaders Need to Think and Act Differently

1. David McRaney, *You Are Not So Smart* (New York: Avery, 2011).
2. "2015 Social CEO Report," CEO.com, http://www.ceo.com/social-ceo-report-2015/.
3. "How Millennials Use and Control Social Media," American Press Institute, March 16, 2015, http://www.americanpressinstitute.org/publications/reports/survey-research/millennials-social-media/.
4. "GE's Jeff Immelt on Digitizing in the Industrial Space," McKinsey, October 2015, http://www.mckinsey.com/insights/organization/ges_jeff_immelt_on_digitizing_in_the_industrial_space.

INDEX

ACKNOWLEDGMENTS

Call it a clan, call it a network, call it a tribe, call it a family.
Whatever you call it, whoever you are, you need one.

—Jane Howard, author

This book has been a network journey of its own. Our team of individuals and partner organizations is diverse and spread around the world—from our writers in Boston, Dallas, and Philadelphia, to our editor in California, to our researcher in Brazil and our technologists in South Africa, Malaysia, and Romania. Connected by technology, and each bringing unique expertise and perspectives, we have come together to tell the story of network creation and network value.

We are grateful not only to the individuals who have brought this research and writing to fruition but also to the institutional partners who have supported us on this journey, including the SEI Center at the Wharton School of Business; Mukul Pandya, managing editor at Knowledge@Wharton; and the entire Harvard Business Review Press team, including Editorial Director Tim Sullivan, Senior Editor Gardiner Morse, Associate Publisher Keith Pfeffer, and Marketing Communications Director Julie Devoll.

Lastly, we want to acknowledge all our friends and family members who have listened to our every story along the way and have lent their own networks to ensure that we correctly told the story of network creation and value.

Barry Libert's Acknowledgments

I wish to thank the following (in alphabetical order).

Tom Alden, for his amazing friendship, intellectual insights, and deeply considered systems and frameworks.

Rob Barber, who has been a client of mine for many years, a thoughtful CEO, and an early adopter of my insights and recommendations.

Megan Beck, whose talents never cease to amaze me and who has used her brilliant mind and expansive heart to write bravely, unceasingly, and energetically to bring these ideas into practical, inspiring expression.

Donna Carpenter and Maurice Coyle, who taught me the difference between prescriptive and descriptive writing.

Cecily Cassum, Cari Ryding, and Maureen Walsh, who shared their ideas about kindness and its importance to our every action, especially in the networked world.

Les Charm, who stuck by me when I lost my way and reminded me what was important in life and in business.

Meryl Comer, who understood the moment I met her that networks are the future of health care reform.

Arnie Cohen, a thoughtful relative and psychologist, who has spent the last thirty years discussing with me the intersection of business and personal attitudes and insights.

Susan Corso, who is a great friend and partner as well as an amazing author in her own right, and whose clear thinking and thoughtful words have touched every page of this book.

Geoff D'Arcy, who is a true philosopher, historian, friend, and storyteller without whom I could not have done this book.

Glenn Kramon, senior editor of the *New York Times*, who gave me the chance twenty years ago to write my first op-ed on these issues for the *Times*, along with Jon Hilsenrath at the *Wall Street Journal*, who let me voice these same thoughts in the *WSJ*.

Michael Krugman, who is the vice president of technology of Boston University and the smartest historian and greatest technologist I know; he is also a dear friend.

Vivian Polikar, who is a brilliant consultant who has supported our research efforts for the past two years.

Steve Potter, who is the US managing partner of Odgers Berndtson, an international search firm, and who originally tried to hunt my head for a hedge fund in 1991 and, since then, has partnered with me every step along the way.

Bill Ribaudo, who is the TMT leader of Deloitte, whom I met more than twenty years ago, when I first started communicating the ideas contained in this book; he remained a loyal friend and supporter when no one else did.

Alex Roth, for his constant exchange of ideas and critical thinking; as head of strategy at Informa, he is working daily to implement these ideas globally.

Doug Ward and George Calapai, who have created a digital platform that encompasses everything contained herein.

Terry Waters, whom I met ten years ago and who has continued to push the envelope of subscription revenue models.

Jerry Wind, who believes in the power of networks and who has tirelessly worked to bring that message to the world.

John Winsor, who, as founder and chairman of Victor and Spoils, fully appreciates the power of networks and the difficulty of creating and nourishing them.

All my clients, and the CEOs of large and small organizations that I have served over the past thirty years. I cannot name you all. But those that require special note are Terri Ludwig, Charlie Werhane, Pradip Sitaram, and Craig Mellendick of Enterprise. They were willing to share their story so that others can benefit.

Finally, I want to thank my family. I have adored my wife, Ellen, from the moment I met her thirty-three years ago. She has supported me since I first developed these concepts in the late 1990s.

My boys, Michael and Adam, whom I love dearly. You have taught my peers and me how to live and share what we have, do, and know in the network age. And my dad, who, at ninety, is amazing and tech-savvy. You give me hope that one day, I can be as kind and as gentle and as good a role model as you have been.

May the power of the network be with all of you!

Megan Beck's Acknowledgments

Andy Fenley, my delightful husband, who has supported me on many dramatic changes and crazy ideas over the years. I am glad that we are able to change together.

Sylvie Fenley, my dear daughter, who every day shows me that time is precious—both scarce and beautiful—and that we need to focus on what really matters.

My parents and sisters, Steve, Judy, Maureen, and Heather, my first and most important network, the one that provided the foundation for everything else—and still does!

Barry Libert, a man with big ideas and great kindness who invited me to partner with him on this adventure and created space for me to contribute exactly as I wanted.

Susan Corso, a woman of too many talents, whose thought partnership, wise words, and great spirit improved this book and our journey immeasurably.

Vivian Polikar, our meticulous and thoughtful researcher.

My wonderful advisers and mentors at Bain & Company—Michael Brookshire, Ossa Fisher, Hernan Saenz, and Lauren Sacha—and particularly Aaron Miller, with whom I learned a lot about business, management, and creating change.

Three great professors who taught me wonderful things (from computer science, to writing, to finance) and believed in me at key times in my life: Alan Cline, Robert King, and Andres Almazan.

Isaac Barchas, director of the Austin Technology Incubator, where I got my first real taste of entrepreneurship.

I hope to pass on the knowledge, wisdom, and generosity that you have shared with me many times over.

Jerry Wind's Acknowledgments

Barry Libert, the lead author of this book, has been a tireless advocate of digital networks ever since we met fifteen years ago. I had the pleasure of publishing Barry's breakthrough book *We Are Smarter Than Me* when I was the editor of Wharton School Publishing, and it has had a significant impact on me and my pursuits.

Al West Jr., the founding CEO and chairman of SEI, who encouraged the establishment of the center with the express intention to be a catalyst for change and challenge the conventional theory and definition of the firm.

Victor Fung and William Fung, the architects and long-term leaders of the innovative Li & Fung network, which consists of more than fifteen thousand factories in more than forty countries and was the basis for the book *The Network Challenge*.

In addition, I want to thank the second generation of leaders, Spencer Fung, the current CEO of Li & Fung; and Sabrina Fung, who leads the Fung Retail Group. They continue to push the concepts of network orchestration.

Paul Kleindorfer, my close, late colleague and collaborator on *The Network Challenge* conference and book, which brought together numerous network researchers from diverse disciplines. I miss him personally and professionally.

In addition, I want to thank my clients: the brave leaders of the firms I consulted with and who have been willing to experiment with innovative network concepts.

Wharton's Future of Advertising Innovation Network and Catharine Hays, who contributed the concept of all touch point orchestration, the cornerstone of our forthcoming book *Beyond Advertising*.

The many students and executives whom I have taught and who have been my reverse mentors.

My colleagues, who provide the intellectual climate that encourages challenging the well-accepted theory of the firm.

And finally, the network of my family, who have provided continuous support and encouragement to all my professional, pro bono, and other fun activities.

Thank you all! You have been the network that supported me throughout everything.

ABOUT THE AUTHORS

BARRY LIBERT is Chairman and CEO of OpenMatters and a Senior Fellow at the Wharton School's SEI Center, the world's first think tank for management education. Libert also serves on the boards of several companies, providing business model and platform expertise, and has been a strategic adviser to the leaders of such companies as AT&T, Microsoft, GE Healthcare, Deloitte, ESPN, and Goldman Sachs. He has spent the last fifteen years investing in digital start-ups (social, mobile, and cloud). His portfolio companies manage digital networks for more than three hundred brands. His passion is researching business models and value, and he has written and lectured extensively on this topic. He holds a BA from Tufts University and an MBA from Columbia Business School. He lives in Boston and is happily married and the father of two grown sons.

MEGAN BECK is the Chief Insights Officer at OpenMatters, where she leads research, publications, and curriculum initiatives. She is also an associate on network initiatives at the Wharton SEI Center. Megan is a former consultant and spent several years at Bain & Company before leaving to advise clients directly in her areas of expertise, including digital technology, entrepreneurship, and human capital management. A longtime Longhorn, she received a BA in the Plan II Honors Program at the University of Texas at Austin, as well as a BS in computer science. She holds an MBA from the McCombs School of Business.

JERRY (YORAM) WIND is the Lauder Professor and Professor of Marketing at the Wharton School and the founding director of the SEI Center for Advanced Studies in Management. He is internationally

known for pioneering research on networked organizations, leadership mental models, and marketing strategy. He consults with major firms around the world, providing expert testimony, and has lectured at over fifty universities worldwide. He has authored more than two dozen books on various topics, including network theory, innovation, and leadership.

OPENMATTERS is a data science company. It focuses on analyzing business models and the underlying sources of value. The firm harnesses technology, big data and analytics to categorize and measure business model performance. OpenMatters uses proprietary research to build indices and ratings for investors and strategies and rankings for companies to help both achieve better returns.

THE WHARTON SEI CENTER for Advanced Studies in Management is the world's first think tank for management education. The SEI Center ensures the relevance of management research and teaching to the evolving needs of business and society in the twenty-first century by joining with global thought leaders in diverse fields to anticipate the needs of management, identify forces of change, and understand emerging management paradigms.